Starting and Operating a Child Care Center

Starting and Operating a Child Care Center

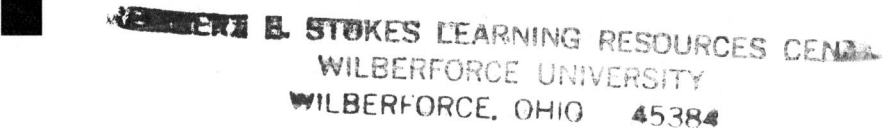

Jean **B**illman
Winona State University

Madison, Wisconsin • Dubuque, Iowa • Indianapolis, Indiana
Melbourne, Australia • Oxford, England

Book Team

Editor *Paul L. Tavenner*
Production Editor *Jayne Klein*

Brown & Benchmark
A Division of Wm. C. Brown Communications, Inc.

Vice President and General Manager *Thomas E. Doran*
Executive Managing Editor *Ed Bartell*
Executive Editor *Edgar J. Laube*
Director of Marketing *Kathy Law Laube*
National Sales Manager *Eric Ziegler*
Marketing Manager *Pamela Cooper*
Advertising Manager *Jodi Rymer*
Managing Editor, Production *Colleen A. Yonda*
Manager of Visuals and Design *Faye M. Schilling*

Production Editorial Manager *Vickie Putman Caughron*
Publishing Services Manager *Karen J. Slaght*
Permissions/Records Manager *Connie Allendorf*

Wm. C. Brown Communications, Inc.

Chairman Emeritus *Wm. C. Brown*
Chairman and Chief Executive Officer *Mark C. Falb*
President and Chief Operating Officer *G. Franklin Lewis*
Corporate Vice President, Operations *Beverly Kolz*
Corporate Vice President, President of WCB Manufacturing *Roger Meyer*

Cover design by Sailer & Cook Creative Services

Interior design by Jeanne Regan

Cover photo by Bob Coyle

Copyedited by Laurie McGee

Copyright © 1993 by Wm. C. Brown Communications, Inc. All rights reserved

Library of Congress Catalog Card Number: 92-70044

ISBN 0-697-14550-6

No part of this publication may be reproduced, stored in a retrieval system, or transmitted, in any form or by any means, electronic, mechanical, photocopying, recording, or otherwise, without the prior written permission of the publisher.

Printed in the United States of America by Wm. C. Brown Communications, Inc., 2460 Kerper Boulevard, Dubuque, IA 52001

10 9 8 7 6 5 4 3 2 1

To all the present and future child care center directors who strive diligently to provide quality programs for young children and their families.

CONTENTS

Preface xi

CHAPTER 1 INTRODUCTION 1

How to Use This Workbook 2
   The Group Approach 2
   The Simulation Approach 3
The Student/Group Member's Role 3
   Evaluating Student Performance 4
The Instructor's Role 5

CHAPTER 2 GETTING STARTED 9

Initial Planning 10
   Making Decisions About Your Child Care Center 10
   Purposes, Goals, and Philosophy Statements 12
Reaching the Public 14
   Naming the Center 14
   Needs Assessment/Market Research 14
   Informational Brochure 15

CHAPTER 3 MANAGEMENT STRUCTURES 27

Program Sponsorship 28
   Publicly Run Programs 28
   Privately Run Programs 29
Establishing and Working With A Board 29
   Board of Directors/Advisory Board Members 29
   Orientation of New Board Members 30
   Articles of Incorporation/Bylaws 31

CHAPTER 4 STAFFING THE CENTER 39

Hiring Staff Members 40
   Job Descriptions 40
   Recruiting 41
   Application Form 41
   Screening Applicants 42
   Checking References 42
   Interviewing 42
   Second Interviews 43
Coordinating Staff Duties 44
   Staffing Schedules 44
   Orientation 44
   Substitutes 44

CHAPTER 5 SUPERVISION, EVALUATION, AND TRAINING OF STAFF 61

Staff Management 62
   Staff Meetings 62
   Staff Training 63
   Evaluating Staff 65
   Termination 66
   Supervising Staff 66
Written Records 67
   Personnel Policies 67
   Personnel Records 69
Professional Development 70
   Early Childhood Professional Organizations 70
   A Code of Ethics 70
   Advocacy 71

CHAPTER 6   FINANCIAL AND LEGAL CONSIDERATIONS   85

Building and Equipping the Center   86
   Start-Up Costs   86
   Furnishing A Classroom   86
Managing Finances   87
   The Operating Budget   87
   Income   89
   Making Purchases   90
   Raising Money   91
   Grant Proposals   91
   Bookkeeping   93
Legal Requirements   93

CHAPTER 7   PHYSICAL SPACE NEEDS FOR THE CENTER   111

Planning the Center   112
   Locating the Center   112
   State and Local Building Regulations   112
   Leasing Space versus Building   113
The Effects of the Physical Environment on the Children and Staff   113

CHAPTER 8   THE CHILDREN'S PROGRAM   123

Planning the Curriculum   124
Writing a Child Care Plan   126
Children's Records   128

CHAPTER 9   HEALTH AND SAFETY IN THE CENTER   141

Keeping the Children and Staff Safe and Healthy   142
   The Need for a Written Plan   142
   Emergency and Accident Policies   142
   Health Policies   144
   Staff Health   145
Health Care Consultants   146
   Health and Safety in the Curriculum   146

CHAPTER 10   NUTRITION AND MEALS   155

Planning the Food Program   156
   Child and Adult Care Food Program   156
   Menu Planning   156
   Food Resource Management   156
   Mealtimes   157
Special Food Problems   159
   Celebrations   159
   Other Nutritional Concerns   159

CHAPTER 11   WORKING WITH PARENTS   173

The Relationship Between the Center and the Family   174
   The Director and Parents   174
   Parental Involvement   175
   Responding to Parents' Concerns and Feelings   175
   Cultural Diversity   175
Communicating with Parents   176
   Information for Parents   176
   The Intake Process/Preenrollment Interview   178
   Parent-Teacher Conferences   179
   Parent Meetings   180
Other Ways to Involve Parents   181
   A Social/Family Worker   182

CHAPTER 12   MARKETING YOUR PROGRAM   197

Marketing Suggestions   198

CHAPTER 13   EVALUATION IN CHILD CARE PROGRAMS   211

The Use of Evaluation in Child Care Programs   212
   Summative and Formative Evaluation   212
   Finding a Focus for Evaluation   212
   The Evaluation Process   212
Types of Evaluation Commonly Used in Child Care Programs   213
   Group Evaluation   213
   Program Evaluation   213
   Meeting Licensing Requirements   214
   Accreditation   215

APPENDIX A	STATE LICENSING AND CERTIFICATION AGENCIES 225	APPENDIX C	THE NATIONAL ASSOCIATION FOR THE EDUCATION OF YOUNG CHILDREN'S CODE OF ETHICAL CONDUCT 237
APPENDIX B	EARLY CHILDHOOD PROFESSIONAL ORGANIZATIONS AND INFORMATION SOURCES 231	APPENDIX D	SUGGESTED MATERIALS LIST 245

Index   249

PREFACE

This workbook is designed to be used in an undergraduate course in the Administration of Early Childhood Programs. It can be used, however, by others interested in designing an early childhood program. Institutions of higher education need to offer courses that include training in skills such as licensing process, budgeting, personnel management, and compliance monitoring (Slavenas, R. 1990, *Journal of Early Childhood Teacher Education* 11(2): 16–19). Directors of child care programs in Illinois rated these areas of competency as more important to their role than the curriculum planning and child development courses that are traditionally offered in most college programs.

With this workbook students simulate the processes that a group would actually go through in setting up an early childhood program (in this case, a child care center). In addition, students will actually do some of the many administrative tasks that they will need to know as directors of programs for young children: budgeting; personnel management; curriculum monitoring; evaluating programs; marketing; working with families; and scheduling. The outstanding feature of this workbook approach is that almost all the work is done in small cooperative-learning groups during class time. All decision making is done through group discussion. All students share equally in data gathering and in producing documents to add to the final product—a folio of the group's work. This book is also designed so that each student is evaluated both for individual work and his or her contribution to the group.

This workbook can be used in conjunction with another textbook that contains the theories and research base for managing early childhood programs. If students have access to several textbooks, they can use them as references, but do their in-class work using this workbook. It can also be used alone when the content material is supplied by short lectures by the instructor.

This workbook requires students to have a copy of their state's licensing requirements. Many of the exercises in the workbook will help students become familiar with the regulations governing child care centers in their particular state. Examples in the workbook are taken from the requirements of several different states, but students will be urged to consult their own state's guidelines whenever possible. (In the Slavenas study, 88% of the directors felt knowledge of state licensing requirements was an essential skill.)

The workbook is itself a selection of exercises that need to be performed in setting up an actual program. Worksheets are included at the end of each chapter to be used with the exercises in the text. Instructors could further select which activities their students would perform.

Although this workbook is intended to teach the *process* of administration, students come away with a *product*—the folio they have helped their group create. Former students report that they have impressed potential employers with it at interviews. One graduate, now a director of a campus child care center, said that her folio resembles a tattered teddy bear and goes everywhere with her.

In planning for a child care center, students and other planners must consider theories about how children develop and learn, the needs of families and the community, and their own background and abilities. This workbook helps students synthesize what they have learned through early childhood coursework and practicum experiences. The group process forces participants to look at the outcomes that will result from different policy statements they make or operational procedures they set up. Working together to complete the exercises in this workbook should enable early childhood students and other planners to learn the basic collaborative and administrative tasks involved in starting and operating a variety of programs for young children.

Acknowledgments

I wish to thank several people who helped me with ideas and suggestions in preparing this workbook. My early childhood students at Winona State University field-tested nearly all the exercises in this workbook and insisted that I learn to give clear directions. Diane Aegler, one of my graduate students, encouraged me to write this book. My friend Pam Eyden, a free-lance writer, gave suggestions for preparing the prospectus. Ruth Doocy, director of the Winona State University Child Care Center, gave me feedback on the first draft of the early chapters. Dr. Jan Sherman, my colleague at WSU, made corrections in the final draft and suggested a format for the exercises. My husband, Milo, patiently read through several drafts and let me know where the writing was confusing. Krystal Himmler gave invaluable help by teaching me how to use the word processor. Steve Hermann and Rob Sklenar of the WSU Photo Services provided most of the photographs. To them all, I express my appreciation of their expertise and thanks for their help.

The following reviewers helped me to clarify certain points and enlarge on others:

Patricia Ainsa, Ph.D.
University of Texas-El Paso

Richard Elardo, Ph.D.
University of Iowa

Professor Joyce Keillor
Greenville College

Jean Billman

1

INTRODUCTION

Chapter Outline

How to use this workbook

The student/group member's role

Summary

The instructor's role

References

How to Use This Workbook

The Group Approach

This workbook is set up to help you learn the administrative and social skills you will need to start and operate a program for young children. Ideally, you will be carrying out the exercises with others. They could be classmates in a college course, parents who want to start a playgroup for their children, community members who want a preschool in their neighborhood, corporation executives who are planning an on-site day care center, or public school personnel who are planning a program to serve at-risk four-year-olds. All groups should have at least one member who has some background and experience in early childhood education and has a good knowledge of developmentally appropriate practice for young children.

The cooperative-learning-groups approach used here is based on the research of Dr. Roger T. Johnson, professor of curriculum and instruction, and his brother, Dr. David W. Johnson, professor of educational psychology, who both teach at the University of Minnesota. They believe that students can learn more if they are actively engaged in their own learning. "In order to maximize their achievement, especially when studying conceptually complex and content-dense material, college-level students should not be allowed to be passive while they are learning. One way to get students more actively involved in this process is to structure cooperative interaction into college classes so that students have to explain what they are learning to each other, learn each other's point of view, give and receive support from classmates, and help each other dig below the superficial level of understanding of the material they are learning" (Johnson, Johnson, and Smith 1990, 11).

The benefits of using cooperative learning groups are many. Johnson and Johnson (1987) did a meta-analysis of all the studies that had been conducted on the effects of cooperative learning on student achievement, feelings, and attitudes and found the results to be universally positive. They were able to document the following outcomes:

1. Competition is dramatically lowered. Students actually help each other.

2. Students work to a higher level of achievement. Peer pressure and support help poorer students do better than they would alone.

3. Students have a positive attitude toward the material. They learn it thoroughly and retain it longer. Oral rehearsal is a good way to learn.

4. Students use higher-level thinking skills. They have to think of and consider many alternative ways of solving problems and making decisions.

5. Students like class, instructor, each other, and self better. It also fosters friendship and understanding between male and female, races, able-bodied and disabled. "Cooperativeness was positively related to a number of indices of psychological health, namely emotional maturity, well-adjusted social relations, strong personal identity, and basic trust in and optimism about people" (Johnson and Johnson 1987, 38).

6. Students learn social skills needed to work collaboratively. Many of the people who lose jobs or seem maladjusted in their social relationships have never learned to get along with others. "Many people realize that a college education or vocational training improves their career opportunities, but many are less aware that interpersonal skills may be the set of skills most important to their employability, productivity, and career success. Employers typically value verbal communication, responsibility, initiative, and interpersonal and decision-making skills. A question all employers have in mind when they interview a job applicant is, 'Can this person get along with other people?' Having a high degree of technical competence is not enough to ensure a successful career. A person also has to have a high degree of interpersonal competence" (Johnson and Johnson 1989, 32). The assumption is that the collaborative competencies gained can be successfully applied to other social settings such as career, family, and community.

The Simulation Approach

Doing the exercises in this workbook simulates what any group of people would have to do to start a child care center. Although there may be no actual center, groups will pretend that there is. Indeed, sometimes students get so caught up in planning for their mythical program that it becomes a very real place in their imaginations. Going through the process of having to discuss each policy decision, of writing press releases, of scheduling staff, and so on makes it much easier to do these managerial jobs when it is necessary for a real program. Students feel confident of their abilities. They know that they can carry out most administrative tasks or know where to go to get help. They have also learned what administrators do and understand the process involved in operating any program that involves children and families.

The skills learned in setting up a child care center are easily transferable to any other kind of early childhood program or to any other business.

The Student/Group Member's Role

The cooperative learning approach is a radical departure from the ways many college students have been expected to perform in the past. The competition for grades and the instructor's attention is keen in most college classrooms. Many students have never had to rely on their peers to accomplish assignments.

Early childhood education students often get extensive experience in ways to interact with young children. However, early educators often find when they get jobs in their field, they usually spend more time working with other adults than they do with children. Parents, teachers, maintenance and office staff, media personnel, board members, licensing consultants, bankers, and retailers are just a few of the people an administrator of a child care program has to deal with on an everyday basis. Identifying and carrying out what needs to be done to make the program operate to the benefit of children and their families takes the collaboration of many people. This group approach not only lets you practice the administrative skills you will need, but also gives you experience in using the social skills you must have to be an effective administrator.

Working with others, however, is not easy. In fact, most administrators will tell you that working with adults is sometimes much more difficult than working with children. It is a necessary, and often challenging, part of being a professional early childhood educator or director of a children's program.

Here are some suggestions that might help you in interacting with other group members:

1. Listen to what each one is saying. If you're not sure what they mean, ask them to explain themselves more clearly.

2. Give your views and opinions based on your own knowledge and experiences, but solicit others' views also.

3. Be ready to compromise. Nothing can be accomplished in group work if one member insists on always having his or her own way. Expect others to do the same. In a democracy, the majority rules.

4. The advantage of diverse groups is that they have different talents. Some members will excel in certain areas and have weaknesses in others. Identify each member's strengths and rely on his or her using them for the group. Help those who have difficulty understanding or doing the work. However, you have a right to ask each group member to turn out excellent work. Your group will be preparing a folio (packet or folder) of administrative forms, policies, and papers. Expect that the typing/word processing, chart making, or other assignments that each member does for this group project will meet high standards. Let the person know if it doesn't and ask them to redo it.

5. Be willing to do the reading and research outside of class that will contribute to the goals of your group. This may involve visiting early childhood programs, interviewing

This group is already learning to work together. Singing songs, reciting fingerplays, and telling stories are part of each day for these children. *Photo by the author*

      administrators, looking up information in the library, writing to outside resources for information, or other ways you find to enhance what your group is doing.

6. Try to be there when your group meets. Be flexible about coming to class early or staying late if the group is having trouble finishing all assignments.

Evaluating Student Performance

Using the instructions in this workbook, you and your group will work together to make a folio of materials that will be valuable for anyone who wants to direct a children's program. It will contain the typed policies and statements your group has formulated by following the assigned exercises. (If you are a community group, you will choose yourselves which materials need to be written.) You will make enough copies of the materials so that each group member and the instructor will have a copy.

You will organize the folio in some way so that the material is easily accessible to anyone reading it. This may include use of a table of contents, section dividers, different colored paper for each section, or other ways you find to clarify the topics covered. Following the workbook chapter titles is one simple way to do this. This folio will be given a group grade. While the *product* that you put together should be done well, the *process* your group goes through in discussing the issues and making decisions will be even more important to you in your career as an administrator of children's programs.

Your instructor will evaluate your ability to function cooperatively in a group endeavor as well as the quality of the materials in the folio. She or he may ask you to evaluate your own group performance and that of other group members. You will also be given individual assignments to complete. These will be graded based on your work alone. Ask your instructor to explain the grading system.

Note. Although men and women can be and are directors of centers, in this workbook directors are referred to by the feminine pronoun.

In this workbook the terms teacher or child care worker are used to refer to those who care directly for the children. The assumption is that the teaching staff of most child care centers have wide differences in educational background and experience. Some may have bachelor's or advanced degrees in early childhood education; others may have had no formal education or training beyond what they get on the job.

Summary

While producing an administrative folio you will have an opportunity to get to know a small group of your peers well. You will also learn what processes are involved in running a children's program. Additionally, you will have many opportunities to practice and examine the interpersonal skills you will need to be an effective administrator. Children's programs need knowledgeable, competent leadership from those who understand young children and know how to work effectively with other adults.

The Instructor's Role

The instructor or facilitator should form the groups. At least initially, avoid self-chosen groups as they tend to be homogeneous.

Find the size group that works well for you. This could be pairs, trios, or quads. Kabel (1990) felt that groups of three to five were best, "with four being often the ideal number" (1). A group of five seems to slow the progress and doesn't allow enough opportunity for students to practice their oral skills. Pairs of two and three often don't get enough different viewpoints for a good discussion. A group of four can easily be subdivided for particular task completion. Of course, sometimes not all groups can have four members. In that case, experiment with three and five to see which feels most comfortable.

Assign groups randomly. If it's a group of students whose capabilities you know, structure groups. Strive for diversity of gender, race/ethnicity, abilities, ages, and experience. According to Johnson and Johnson (1986) heterogeneous groups have the potential for the most power. They have developed some innovative strategies for grouping (Johnson and Johnson 1985). (I have students put their names on pieces of paper and place them in a box. The student who has the next birthday or the youngest brother starts the drawing and groups of four are picked at random. Some groups may have five members. If I have several graduate students in a class of undergraduates, I may ask that only one graduate student be in a group. I also arrange special times for the graduate students to work together as their own group on specific graduate projects.)

Whenever possible, arrange the physical environment to make it easier for people to work together. Sitting around a table or putting desks together in a cluster helps define the group and makes everyone feel a part of it. Ask each group to include an empty chair or desk for the instructor/facilitator.

During the early phases of group deliberations assign roles so groups can monitor their own inner workings. These are some suggested roles the instructor/facilitator might use (Johnson and Johnson 1987):

1. **Facilitator**—helps define what the group will be working on and keeps the group on task.

2. **Recorder**—takes notes of decisions the group makes and writes them up so all can have copies.

3. **Encourager**—gives positive reinforcement for contributions, tries to get people to elaborate on their ideas, and makes each member feel important to the group.

4. **Observer**—sits back from the group and *silently* records how often each contributes to the group's discussions and gives the group feedback on how well they are collaborating and where they might improve.

5. **Summarizer/checker**—at the end of the session goes over what the group has accomplished and talks about what else needs to be done.

These roles can be rotated during the first few sessions until the groups are functioning smoothly.

Try to schedule the class or meeting so that it is uninterrupted and lasts at least two hours. Meeting once a week for two and a half hours is preferable to three 50-minute sessions. It takes time for groups to get settled and working. The group also needs sustained time to make progress. Because each member of the group is actively engaged in helping to solve challenging problems, this can be an intense learning experience. Although on some college campuses it might be possible for students to meet as a group outside of class time, do not make that a requirement of the course. Those who work during the day and commute from long distances would not be able to participate. Encourage the group to divide up the tasks to be accomplished during the week and to bring their completed portions to the group at the next class for group approval or suggestions for improvement.

The role of the instructor for this course is not that of the typical college instructor. She or he becomes more a facilitator or resource person for the group/groups. Thus, he or she makes certain that the group/groups understand the tasks to be accomplished, the purposes of working in groups, and the outcomes that are to be achieved. In clarifying the assignments, however, no more than one-third of the session should be lecture. In a college course the instructor/facilitator may ask students to read chapters in a textbook or articles on administering children's programs *before* they discuss it in their small groups. Each group will decide when it needs more information. Groups may send their own members out to do research. Or they may let the facilitator know what data they need. The facilitator makes resources available to them in the form of model policy statements, documents, statistics, reference materials, samples of budgets, or other materials as they request them. (I have purposely not included models that could be used by students. Students should think through what *they* want to include before seeing how others have done it. However, it would be a good idea for the instructor to have copies of materials available from several different sources so that students could consult them *after* they have first struggled to make up their own. It is more important that they gain confidence in their own abilities to write policies than that they have them written the "right" way.)

The instructor/facilitator discusses the collaborative skills to be learned from this group approach. Getting to know and trust each other, communicating accurately and unambiguously, accepting and supporting one another, and resolving conflicts constructively are all necessary for successful group work (Johnson and Johnson 1989). Being able to voice and defend a point of view, knowing when to compromise, learning to disagree and take criticism without taking it personally, and displaying common courtesy are important to success in any job. The group must see the usefulness of these interpersonal and small-group skills and learn to recognize them when they occur. "Students have to practice cooperative skills long enough to go through the stages of awkward enactment, phony (role-playing) enactment, and mechanical use of the skill to automatic, routine use where the skill is fully internalized" (Johnson and Johnson 1990, 30). For instance, it might seem awkward for the encourager to use phrases such as "Good idea," "You explained that concept well," or "I like the way you shared your experiences in day care with us today" without seeming insincere. With time and practice, however, these efforts at encouragement can become more natural and make the person contributing feel appreciated. Take time to discuss the skills to be learned. Then, spend time sitting in with groups and pointing out examples of what you see the group doing right. Give encouragement whenever appropriate.

If this workbook is being used in a classroom situation, don't rely exclusively on group efforts. Set up a grading system that is based about half on group product and process, but also have individual assignments and one or two tests over required readings and lecture materials. Make this system known from the start. (The grading system I have devised is based half on group participation and half on individual effort. On a 100-point basis students can earn up to 25 points on the group grade for their completed folio. The 25 points for group participation are based on how students are rated by others in their group, their own assessment of their work, and by my evaluation of their contribution. Students are asked to rate themselves and others on the following criteria: (1) how many times the student missed class, (2) how much each contributed to the group discussions (below average, average, above average), (3) how much research, interviewing, reading, visiting centers, and so on each did, (4) how much work outside of class each did (word processing, duplicating, collating, etc.), and (5) how well each used good group skills to accomplish the work of the group (getting along, compromising, being respectful, etc.). In addition students are given several assignments to complete on their own. The four-week menu plan is worth 5 points, the floor plan counts 10 points, the synopsis of three articles on the administrator's role is worth 15 points, and the final examination over reading assignments in their textbook is valued at 20 points.)

There are some pitfalls to keep in mind when using this group approach, however. Kagan (1989) pointed out that it is difficult for teachers to change their ways of teaching, so they might want to start slowly and introduce cooperative learning skills on a piecemeal basis until they get more proficient. Kagan also suggested that teachers who want to use this approach band together and give each other "formal and informal collegial coaching and support" (15).

Sometimes groups simply don't work. Intervene when possible. Tell them again what you expect and suggest some ways they could work together more effectively. Often groups (like dysfunctional families) become expert at hiding their problems. Asking students to rate their own role in the group and that of other members midquarter (using the form on page 8) or about a third of the way into a semester can often reveal problems. They can be asked to rate their effectiveness and that of their teammates on a scale of 1 to 6 (from least to most effective) on such items as sharing information, soliciting ideas and information from others, giving directions and defining tasks, checking for understanding of group members, and showing respect for other's opinions. They are free to make comments about the group's functioning, which only the instructor will read. These comments will be kept confidential but will pinpoint sources of friction within the group that the instructor may need to help the group overcome.

On rare occasions a group member can become discouraged and refuses to participate. Occasionally, a student with a strong personality can try to dominate and control the group. You may need to intervene by speaking in private to persons who seem to have difficulty relating to the cooperative group approach.

One other possible drawback to using this method is that when the groups are working effectively, the instructor has little to do. Groups must have time to do their work. This means that the instructor must keep lectures to a minimum. When groups are engaged in their tasks the instructor can evaluate individual assignments, observe what each group is doing by sitting in silently, or simply be available to answer questions. Sometimes groups get stuck on a certain problem that they are unable to resolve. Moving them on to another topic or giving them ways to resolve the conflict can help the group to accomplish its work. However, as much as possible, the instructor/facilitator should resist interfering. Groups can be very creative about solving their own problems. The students learn more by *doing* these exercises than by listening to an instructor *tell* them how. (Of all the early childhood courses I teach, students report learning most in this one.)

All in all, the benefits to students far outweigh the problems. Using cooperative learning groups is a powerful teaching strategy for helping students learn administrative and social skills they will need to work together effectively in setting up and operating good early childhood programs.

References

Johnson, D. W., and R. T. Johnson. 1985. *Cooperative learning: Warm-ups, grouping strategies, and group activities.* Edina, MN: Interaction Book Company.

———. 1986. *Circles of learning: Cooperation in the classroom (revised).* Edina, MN: Interaction Book Company.

———. 1987. *Learning together and alone: Cooperative, competitive, and individualistic learning.* Englewood Cliffs, NJ: Prentice-Hall.

———. 1989. Social skills for successful group work. *Educational Leadership* 47: 29–33.

Johnson, R. T., D. W. Johnson, and K. A. Smith. 1990. Cooperative learning: An active learning strategy for the college classroom. *Baylor Educator* 15(2): 11–16.

Kabel, R. L. 1990. Cooperative learning and college teaching: Tips from the trenches. *The Teaching Professor* 4(5): 1–2.

Kagan, S. 1989. The structural approach to cooperative learning. *Education Leadership* 47: 12–15.

Midterm Evaluation

How Well Is Your Group Working Together?

List the names of the people in your group. In the appropriate space rate each group member's effectiveness. A rating of 6 is the highest possible rating and indicates that the group member is extremely effective in this area. A 1 rating means the group member is extremely ineffective in this area.

- A. Gives information and opinions to the group
- B. Seeks ideas and opinions from other group members
- C. Focuses the group on the tasks, gives directions, defines roles
- D. Summarizes what the group has accomplished
- E. Brings energy to the group, makes other members feel good
- F. Fulfills his/her responsibilities outside of class

Names	A	B	C	D	E	F	Total

Additional comments about individual contributions or group functioning.

These scores and comments will be kept confidential and will only be used to help the group improve its interaction.

2

GETTING STARTED

Chapter Outline

Initial planning

Reaching the public

Summary

References

Assignments

2.1 Make a chart of children's programs.

2.2 Brainstorm ideas for your center.

2.3 Make purposes, goals, and philosophy statements.

2.4 Name the center.

2.5 Design a one-page needs assessment survey form.

2.6 Rate several brochures after developing criteria.

2.7 Write an informational brochure for your program.

Initial Planning

Early childhood programs come in a variety of different forms. This chapter will help you decide what kind of program your group will develop. Some of the programs that might be found in a typical community are family day care, child care center, nursery school, Montessori school, Head Start, public school preschool, home-visitor program, a demonstration school in a teacher-training institution, family or parent education program, resource and referral program, church-sponsored program, classes for special needs infants, toddlers, and preschoolers, parent cooperatives, latch-key programs, and corporation-sponsored programs.

2.1 Make a chart. For each type of program previously listed identify a program in your community that best meets each of these labels and provide the following information: person in charge, number of children served, ages of children, hours, sponsor and/or funding sources, and a short description of the program.

All of these programs are administered by someone. They all require planning, operating, staffing, leading, monitoring, and evaluating. Someone is making administrative decisions and policies that shape how each program is run. When a person has a background of training and experience in child development and early childhood education, he or she can exert leadership of child care programs in such a way that they are beneficial to young children and their families (Kuykendall 1990).

In some communities parents have many different types of children's programs from which to choose. From such a variety they are able to pick a program that matches their needs and life-style. As family sizes have become smaller and children have fewer siblings, parents may want a program that meets only a few hours a week that helps their child learn to get along with other age-mates. They may be looking for a drop-in center where they can leave their children for a few hours a week while they go to the dentist or shopping. They may prefer a family/parent education program where they can participate with their child on a once-a-week basis. If both parents work outside the home, as they do in the majority of young families, they may need full-time child care. In a community that has a diversity of early childhood programs, location, cost, scheduling, and curriculum are considerations that parents must weigh before enrolling their children.

In a country that is facing a child care crisis, many locations have limited child care options. Parents are often forced to settle for less-than-ideal arrangements for their children because more and better programs for young children are needed in most communities.

The greatest need is for quality child care programs for children of working parents. The number of women with young children who are in the labor force has risen dramatically in the last twenty years. According to the National Commission on Working Women (Jensen and Chevalier 1990), in 1986, 49 percent of mothers of children one year and younger were working. This percentage rose as the children got older until 65 percent of mothers of 5-year-olds were working outside the home. One out of every five mothers in the work force was maintaining her own family.

Realizing that the same or similar administrative processes would be required for other children's programs, this book focuses on the director's job in a child care center. The skills learned in these exercises are easily transferable to other types of educational programs or to other positions that require administrative skills.

Making Decisions About Your Child Care Center

Your group will be creating a hypothetical child care center. You will make decisions about the size, location, age-range, grouping patterns, housing, and equipment for your own specific program.

This toddler is relaxed and happy in her caregiver's lap. The teacher shows her own pleasure in sharing this moment with her. *Photo by the author*

The sponsorship of the program may vary. Here are several different types of child care sponsors:

1. It could be sponsored by a corporation to meet the child care needs of its employees.
2. Religious groups could operate programs to meet the needs of members and/or to serve the surrounding community.
3. It could be run for profit by one or several owners or a franchise.
4. A college could sponsor a campus child care facility for its students and staff. It might also sponsor a child development center to do research on young children or as a clinical setting for students in training in many fields.
5. It could be part of a public school effort at meeting the developmental needs of a targeted group such as those considered "at-risk" for future learning or those with limited English language proficiency.
6. It could also be a community-based, private, nonprofit center.
7. A hospital might offer a 24-hour center for children of their employees.
8. The city, state, or federal government could operate a center for government employees' dependents.
9. A public school might sponsor before and after school care for children from kindergarten through elementary school.
10. A shopping mall may provide a drop-in center where their customers can leave their children while they are shopping.

You may think of other center-type programs. Family day cares usually operate under a different set of requirements and are not included here even though almost as many young children are cared for in homes (22%) as in centers (23%) (Hofferth 1987).

There are some common requirements for this assignment, however, which all the hypothetical programs shall have in common. All will be in operation for at least ten hours a day. Each program will have its own facility, which is not used by any other group for more than a couple of hours a week. Your program will be guided by the regulations governing child care centers in your state. For a list of the state department responsible for licensing in your state and its address, consult Appendix A.

2.2   Your group will begin to decide what kind of child care program you wish to have. You will need to spend some time just brainstorming the kind of program you want. Try not to have the same kind of center as another group. Everyone must contribute ideas. Have one member of your group write these ideas down in any order. It may take several sessions until you can clearly see the full scope of your program.

Purposes, Goals, and Philosophy Statements

After you have some idea of the kind of program you want, you will begin formulating statements of the purposes, goals, and philosophy of your program.

Purposes: Why? Why do you want to offer this service?

Goals: What? What outcomes do you expect to accomplish?

Philosophy: How? How do you propose to operate your program so that you can reach your goals?

2.3   Begin to formulate the purposes, goals, and philosophy statements on the exercise worksheets. Try to define what should go on each one. There should be much discussion because each member of your group will have different views based on his or her own background and experiences. Accept that you may not always agree. You can go back and change your purposes, goals, and philosophies several times in the next few sessions as you clarify ideas by your discussions, and you begin to see some of the limits to what one program can accomplish. Leave room for future drafts as you refine each of these statements.

Your group needs to be clear about their purpose. Limit your purpose statements to three or four sentences. Gross (1987) has said, "The most potent ingredient in organizational effectiveness is a clear sense of purpose shared by every member of the organization. . . . True purpose is always inspiring; if it doesn't motivate and unify all members of the organization, something is off or missing" (25–26). The director and/or the board must be the keepers of the vision and bring staff back to it when they get so caught up in the day-to-day operations that they forget why the program exists.

Goals can differ for the various groups involved. You might have a set of goals for children, parents, staff members, student interns, and employers or franchise owners. What are the results or outcomes that you want to happen to each population as a result of your program? For example, you might wish to ensure that parents miss fewer days of work due to child care problems. Decreases in the absentee rate of employees might be a goal of a program supported by a business.

Caring for Toddlers, who can be very demanding at times, requires energy, patience, and dedication. *Photo by Rob Sklenar*

As you review the philosophy of your program, Decker and Decker (1988) suggested the following questions to help clarify a group's thinking:

1. What theory or theories of early childhood education best describes how young children grow and develop?
2. How will children be grouped? What will influence this decision?
3. What staff positions will be necessary? What qualifications will each have?
4. What kind of classrooms, materials, equipment will be available? How will the center be arranged?
5. What kind of schedule will be needed?
6. How will your program be evaluated?

Although you will not yet have all the answers to these questions, they are all topics that will have to be addressed during the planning.

Reaching the Public

Naming the Center

2.4 After you have at least a preliminary draft of your purposes, goals, and philosophy, your group must come up with a name for your program. This name will be with the program for a long time so you want to choose one that is not too long or complex. Neither do you want it to be "cute" or "trendy." You also do not want a label that will be outdated within a few years. Write down everyone's ideas and see if you can find a name that is agreeable to each member of your group. Be original! Try to find a name that reflects the focus of your program.

Needs Assessment/Market Research

Before you can go any further in the program planning, you will have to see if there are enough families in the vicinity of your projected child care center who would need your services to make it a viable program. It would be ridiculous to plan a program, renovate or build a facility, hire staff, and equip a center and then not be able to operate it because not enough families would utilize it. Although this is hardly likely to happen in most communities because of the great need for child care, in some places there may be other programs that can supply this service to parents more conveniently or more cheaply than you can. You would have a difficult time filling your child care slots.

You could use several sources of information to determine if a need exists for your program. Some are listed below.

1. Census information. The number of children in a certain age bracket is available from your city or county government. This can usually be found in the Planning and Development (or some analogous) Department or will be on file at the local public library.

2. School districts usually have a fairly accurate count of children under the age of five. This is typically broken down by sex and age group. For example, districts could tell you the number of girls and boys between one and two years, between two and three.

3. Public health departments may also know how many families in a certain geographic region might need child care.

4. County social service departments prepare and disseminate data about the need for and availability of child care services. In many communities they also administer funds to purchase services for low-income families and have a regulatory role in approving and licensing centers and family day care homes.

5. Other child care programs could tell you how many families they have on their waiting lists. Though some families may be on more than one list and some may have made alternative arrangements, this information could help you make a decision about the need for your proposed program.

6. Your local or regional branch of the national Child Care Resource and Referral agency may have information about the need for child care in your community.

7. One of the best ways to get a good idea about whether your program would be able to attract enough families who would use it is to do your own survey. This could be targeted to a special group. For example, in a university setting it could be used at registration time to get information on all students who have young children. You could survey employees

at a corporation to see if they would use on-site day care if it were available. Or, you could do a door-to-door canvass in a housing project or a neighborhood. If you are mailing out a survey, it is wise to remember that postage is a big expense and returns are generally only a small percentage.

2.5   Design a one-page needs assessment survey with no more than seven or eight questions. Make these questions easy to answer by using a checklist or circle-the-right-answer-type responses. Tell briefly why you are taking the survey. Have groups exchange and critique this survey form. React to their feedback.

Informational Brochure

One way to inform the public about your program both before you are in operation and once you have opened your doors is to have a brochure that will tell them about your program. At a minimum you would want to include the following information:

1. Ages and numbers of children the program is licensed to serve.
2. Days and hours of operation.
3. The kinds of services offered. A description of the program's philosophy including educational methods, and religious, political, or philosophical basis, if any.

2.6   Look at brochures for several child care programs. Devise a rating form to evaluate them. This might include readability, attractiveness, format, comprehensiveness of information, or some other criteria you set. Compare individual scores to get your group's best and worst examples. Compare these with what other groups have chosen.

2.7   Write an informational brochure for your proposed program. If your state has specific requirements of what should go into this brochure, include those.

You will want to make your brochure as attractive as possible. In real life, you would want to have it professionally printed. You would use good photographs or interesting multicolor illustrations. Your group's brochure should be eye-catching. Because you will not be using photographs, you might want to consider using hand-drawn pictures or computer graphics to add to its aesthetic appeal.

Because you would be printing hundreds of these for wide distribution, you may want to keep costs down by making this a single page printed on both sides. A two- or threefold sheet works well.

You will also want your brochure to be easy to read. Have other group members proofread what you have written before you begin to type it or put it on your word processor. After that, have someone proof it again to make certain it has no spelling, punctuation, or grammatical errors. (All the documents you produce for this course should be letter-perfect.)

Summary

You and your group have begun the process of starting a child care center. You already have some idea of why you want to establish a center, the types of families you will be serving, where you will be located, and your hours of operations. You have chosen a name and set up a market research plan to see if a center is needed in your community. You have done some initial advertising by handing out your brochures. Your child care center is starting to take shape in your mind.

References

Decker, C. A., and J. R. Decker. 1988. *Planning and administering early childhood programs.* Columbus, OH: Merrill.

Gross, S. 1987. The power of purpose. *Child Care Information Exchange* 56: 25–29.

Hofferth, S. L. 1987. *Child care in the United States.* Testimony before the House Select Committee on Children, Youth, and Family. Hearing on American Families in Today's Economy. Washington, DC.

Jensen, M. A., and Z. W. Chevalier. 1990. *Issues and advocacy in early education.* Boston: Allyn and Bacon.

Kuykendall, J. 1990. Child development: Directors shouldn't leave home without it. *Young Children* 45(5): 47–50.

2.1

Complete this chart

Type of Program	Name of Program	Person in Charge	Number of Children Served	Ages of Children	Hours of Operation	Sponsor/ Funding Sources	Short Description of Program
1. Family Day Care							
2. Child Care Center							
3. Nursery School							
4. Montessori School							
5. Head Start							
6. Public School Preschool							
7. Demonstration-Lab Preschool							
8. Family/Parent Education Program							
9. Resource and Referral Program							
10. Church-Sponsored Program							
11. Parent Cooperation							
12. Latch-Key Program							
13. Corporation-Sponsored Child Care							

2.2

Brainstorm what kind of child care program you want. Write down your group's ideas.

2.3.a

Purposes of your child care program.

2.3.b

Goals.

2.3.c

Philosophy.

2.4

Name the Center.

What suggestions were made? What name was chosen?

2.5

Needs assessment survey.

List questions you will ask.

Feedback from another group.

2.6

Rating scale for child care center brochures.

2.7

Informational brochure for your child care program.

3

MANAGEMENT STRUCTURES

Chapter Outline

Program sponsorship

Establishing and working with a board

Summary

References

Assignments

3.1 Write the bylaws for your center.

3.2 Compare your group's bylaws with models. Discuss what changes should be made.

3.3 Read three articles about the director's administrative role and write a two-page synopsis of each. Share the information.

The creative process requires concentration. The joy is in the doing. *Photo by Steve Hermann*

Program Sponsorship

Just as there are a variety of early childhood programs, there are also many different organizational structures. Some child care programs are publicly run; some are private operations. Some programs are under the direction of a single owner/operator. Two or more people may form a partnership and have joint responsibility for the program. A corporation may be set up with a board of directors who make policy and hire a director to actually administer the program. Some privately run programs are nonprofit; some are for-profit.

Publicly Run Programs

Government agencies may run early childhood programs. Head Start is an example of a federally funded program. Public schools that are funded by the state are operating an increasing number of early childhood programs. New York City has a program that is open to all four-year-olds. In Minnesota and Missouri most of the school districts have once-a-week classes for children below kindergarten age while their parents are meeting in discussion groups. Some schools have prekindergarten classes for children with special needs.

Public agencies are expected to implement and adhere to their own regulations. They are generally exempt from meeting state licensing requirements for child care centers.

Privately Run Programs

Many types of children's programs are private. They can be run for profit or be nonprofit. For-profit centers are operated to produce a return on shareholders' investments. Not-for-profit centers are permitted to make a profit also, but whatever monies are accrued above expenses are used to improve salaries, buy more supplies and equipment, or used in other ways that increase the effectiveness of the center. Each state has statutes that govern the three legal forms of private organizations (Federlein 1986).

1. A *sole proprietorship* is owned by one person who is responsible and liable for all actions. That person may be a sole owner-operator or may employ a large staff.

2. A *partnership* has two or more partners. In a general partnership each partner shares equally in the responsibility for the program. In a limited partnership the general partners' legal responsibility has no limit; but a limited partner is responsible only to the extent of his or her original investment. As a limited partner, he or she is not involved in any but financial decision making.

3. A *corporation* is a legal body that can be for-profit or not-for-profit. Board members may come and go, but the corporation remains unless dissolved. Board members are protected from certain liability actions when the program is incorporated with the state. In general, the corporation is "the most appropriate structure for operation of a day care center" (Federlein 1986, 15) because of the advantages and flexibility the law allows corporations.

Franchises or chains for child care centers can be any one of these forms of organizations. Here, the setting up, furnishing, and staff training are likely to be standardized and operated for profit (Decker and Decker 1988).

Establishing and Working With A Board

Board of Directors/Advisory Board Members

No matter what kind of early childhood program it is, the director will need some help and advice. To start with, she will want to find people who are very interested in what she is trying to do. Seeking people who have diverse backgrounds and expertise will help the board to function in many different ways that could be beneficial to the program. For instance, it would be very helpful to find board members who are knowledgeable in the following areas:

1. *Early childhood education.* They could help with defining the philosophy of the center, determining the curriculum, and hiring teachers.

2. *The law.* They could assist in writing the Articles of Incorporation, handle legal and insurance matters, and help write policies that have legal implications. Having a lawyer during the start-up process would be especially helpful. Generally, however, lawyers charge for their services.

3. *Medicine.* Health care professionals could help write emergency and health policies. They could set up and train staff in sanitary procedures. They could also monitor children's health care records and see that all immunizations are up to date.

4. *Finances.* They could help set up the bookkeeping system, work with budgets, contact outside auditors, and help monitor tuition and other sources of income. They might also assist the director in writing grant proposals.

5. *Nutrition.* They could help plan menus and consult about food purchases and preparation. They could also give some training to the kitchen staff about the nutritional needs of young children.

6. *Building trades.* They could help oversee repairs, renovations, and building that is done at the center. They might serve as a liaison to any contractor the center engages. They could also see that maintenance to the building and grounds is satisfactorily carried out.

7. *Public relations.* They could help publicize your program by preparing news releases, helping design brochures, or speaking to groups about the program. They could advise the director on ways to interest the public in what is going on in the center.

8. *Social worker or family educator.* They could help the staff in their work with families. They might set up a referral process for families who have needs beyond what the center can fulfill. They could assist in the planning and carrying out of some of the parent activities.

Although having representatives from each of the professions listed on a single board would be nearly impossible, the director must try to get the best people available to serve. Membership on a board of a children's program is not just an honor; it is a commitment to maintaining and improving the program.

Parents should be included as board members. Some states require that the majority of board members be parents. In a small program, it may be necessary to accept parent volunteers who agree to serve as board members. However, if a center serves more than forty families, it would be more democratic to have parents elect representatives. This would mean forming a nominating committee, getting parents' permission to put their name on the slate, and holding a meeting of all the parents to have an election. All parents should have an equal chance to serve or be on the ballot. Arranging a specific day or hours for balloting may be an alternative way to elect parent representatives. No one has more interest in seeing that the program functions successfully than do parents who have young children in the program. Parents often have the training and expertise sought and are willing to share it because they know it will mean a better program for their own children.

Though in a very small community it may be hard to do, board members should not be related to the staff members. This avoids any situations where there might be a conflict of interest or nepotism.

Whether it is businesspeople, professionals, community people, or parents who agree to be board members, the director will need to spend time and energy supporting the work of the board. Often, she will be the one to give orientation to the new board members. She will write reports for the board to study and will formulate policies for the board to discuss. They will often take her recommendations when action is required to make necessary changes. She will be the liaison person between the board and the staff.

Orientation of New Board Members

New board members will need orientation to their role. They will need a clear understanding of how their role differs from the director's role.

The following chart supplied by Fishhaut (unpublished, used with permission) outlines their duties:*

Responsibilities of the Board

1. The board sets up the corporate or legal existences of the agency and gives it continuity.

2. It selects and appoints the executive director and delegates responsibility to the executive director for administering the agency.

3. It sees that adequate funds are available for financing the agency's operations, including adequate staff, proper working conditions, salaries, and facilities.

---

*Child Care Board of Directors Orientation (unpublished manuscript) Fishhaut, Erna. University of Minnesota.

4. It governs the agency by policies and plans that it determines and approves and that are formulated with the executive and the staff.

5. It accounts for the service of the agency and the expenditure of funds. To be accountable, it makes provisions for proper bookkeeping and auditing; it sets the budget; and it studies reports, asks questions, and keeps informed regarding the agency's activities and its field of service.

6. It represents the agency in the community through presentation of the agency's point of view to formal and informal groups and to government bodies, and by interpretation of the agency's services.

7. It selects its members carefully and uses their talents and skills in behalf of the agency's purpose.

The Executive Director's Responsibilities

1. Plans and participates in the formulation of policies and procedures.

2. Organizes the agency's services and coordinates the work of the board and the staff.

3. Either directly or by delegation, employs and directs staff, supervises, provides training, and gives professional leadership in the field of the agency's service.

4. Prepare budgets and reports and keeps the board informed about the agency's operations and program.

5. Represents the agency professionally in the community and interprets the agency's services.

6. Helps the board members perform their roles as board members.

In addition to the board's responsibilities outlined by Fishhaut, Sciarra and Dorsey (1990) saw the board or advisory council as the arbitrator in grievance procedures when problems between staff and director cannot be resolved without outside help. Neugebauer (1988) has several suggestions that would be very helpful for a director who is trying to maintain a good working relationship between staff and members of the board.

Articles of Incorporation/Bylaws

To incorporate, the center must have an attorney file "Articles of Incorporation" or a "Certificate of Incorporation" with the Secretary of State. An alternative way used in some states requires that these documents be published in area newspapers. These documents will list names and addresses of initial board members, date of annual meeting, name and address of program, and other pertinent information. The Internal Revenue Service also requires filing of this document by all corporations seeking tax-exempt status (Decker and Decker 1988).

3.1 For this course your center will be incorporated. Your group will write a set of bylaws for your program that will tell how the corporation will be governed, how it will conduct business, and how membership is established and changed.

Use the following outline as a guide:

Article I: Name of the organization.

Article II: Sponsorship/Ownership.
This article tells whether the organization is profit or nonprofit. It might also tell who the founders were and what will be done with income earned in excess of expenses.

Article III: Purpose.

Article IV: Goals.

Article V: Address.

Article VI: Enrollment policy.
(Who will be admitted? Ages served? How are vacancies filled? Nondiscrimination clause?)

Article VII: Financial arrangements.

   A. Fees. (How will tuition be determined? Are there charges for registration, insurance? When will discounts be given? Is there scholarship money available? Is there a sliding fee scale?)

   B. Dates of fiscal year.

   C. Budget. (How will the yearly budget be determined?)

   D. Auditing. (The board will be responsible for having the books audited on an annual or biennial basis by an outside auditor.)

Article VIII: Organization and administration.

   A. Membership of Board of Directors. (How many members? How are they chosen? How many shall be parents of children in the program? What will be the terms of office for board members? How will a rotation be set up so the board has continuity? How will vacancies be filled? Will board members be appointed or elected?)

   B. Responsibilities of board members. (What offices will be held? What will be the duties of each officer?)

   C. Meetings. (What provisions are there for an annual meeting? How often will the board meet? Will notices be sent? How many members will constitute a quorum? Where will a file of the minutes of each meeting be kept?)

   D. Line of authority. (Make an organizational chart showing who reports to whom.)

   E. Committees. (What standing committees will there be? How will *ad hoc* committees [those set up temporarily to work on a particular problem such as preparing for the annual meeting or serving on a corporate-giving campaign] be appointed? To whom will committee chairs report?)

Article IX: Staff.

   A. Members. (What are the titles of the different staff positions?)

   B. Health requirements for staff members.

   C. Other requirements.

Article X: Insurance. (What insurance will the program carry? Liability, medical, workman's compensation, other?)

Article XI: Amendments. (How will these be made?)

Article XII: Parliamentary procedure. (How will meetings be conducted?)

3.2 After you have written bylaws for your program, consult those written for other centers. Hildebrand (1990) has a short, but effective sample.

After the Articles of Incorporation and bylaws are prepared and signed at an incorporators' meeting, and copies are filed with the state or advertised as required, the state approves and issues a corporate charter. Now the board members "own" the program and the center is ready to open its doors.

One of the first orders of business for the new board will be to hire a director. The board sets broad general policies and the director carries out the day-to-day operations of the center using the policies as guidelines.

3.3 Find three journal articles that deal with the many aspects of a center director's role. Write a two-page synopsis of each. Share the information you have gained with the whole group or with your own small group. (Some journals to consult are *Child Care Information Exchange, Day Care and Early Education, Childhood Education, Child and Youth Care Forum, Young Children, Child Welfare,* and *Pre-K Today.*)

Summary

You have looked at the different administrative structures that are possible for child care centers and developed bylaws for your corporation. These will allow your program to be incorporated in your state and begin to operate. You understand the difference between the functions of a board/advisory council and those of the administrator of the program.

References

Decker, C. A., and J. R. Decker. 1988. *Planning and administering early childhood programs.* Columbus, OH: Merrill.

Federlein, A. C. 1986. *Legal issues in early childhood centers.* West Bloomfield, MI: Child Development Designs, Inc.

Fishhaut, E. Institute of Child Development, University of Minnesota, unpublished paper, used with permission.

Hildebrand, V. 1990. *Management of child development centers.* New York: Macmillan.

Neugebauer, R. 1988. 20 ideas for improving board/staff relations. *Child Care Information Exchange* 73: 3–5.

Sciarra, D. J., and A. G. Dorsey. 1990. *Developing and administering a child care center.* 2d ed. Albany, NY: Delmar.

3.1

Articles of Incorporation/Bylaws.

3.2

After looking at models of written bylaws, what does your group need to add or change?

3.3

Reports by classmates/group members on the center director's role.

Write down some of the main ideas shared.

4

STAFFING THE CENTER

Chapter Outline

Hiring staff members

Coordinating staff duties

Summary

References

Assignments

4.1　Discuss the hiring and firing procedures in your center.

4.2　Discuss whether jobs will be filled from within.

4.3　Write job descriptions for a toddler teacher and a cook.

4.4　Write a newspaper ad for a teaching position.

4.5　Design an application form for your program.

4.6　Design a reference form for a teaching position.

4.7　Write up interview questions for a teaching position and exchange them with another group. Revise.

4.8　Set up a staffing schedule for all the staff who work with children.

4.9　Make a list of all topics to be covered in the orientation to new staff members.

4.10　Make up a packet of materials that each teacher will have ready for the substitute.

Hiring Staff Members

Your group will set up the process for recruiting and staffing your program. No job is more influential in affecting the quality of the program you direct, because your center is only as good as the care each child receives.

Taking time to find the best people available is extremely important. Most of your budget will go to paying staff salaries. You can prevent many problems that might be caused by indifferent or disgruntled employees later by careful screening of applicants now.

Decide what jobs you will have to fill for your center. You may want to use *differential staffing* with your program personnel. This means that the head teachers will have different qualifications than the assistant teachers or the teacher aides. If you are serving meals, you will need people to plan, cook, and serve them. Maintenance people will be needed to keep the building and grounds clean. If you pick up and deliver children, you will need someone to drive the bus or van. How will volunteers be used? Will you be able to count them in your staff-child ratio?

Become familiar with your state's requirements for the different positions in your center. What qualifications are needed for a head teacher's job? If you serve infants, is it necessary to have a nurse on your staff? Rhode Island requires that the services of a full or part-time social worker be accessible to each center (Rhode Island Department for Children and Their Families 1984). The only requirement in some states is that teaching staff be over eighteen and have completed high school or be working toward equivalency certification. It is important to know this kind of information before you start the hiring process.

Who will do the hiring? In most programs the director hires the staff with help from the personnel committee of the board. In other programs the personnel committee with the help of the director makes recommendations to the board, who make the final decisions as to who will be hired.

4.1 Discuss who will have the final say in hiring and firing in your program.

4.2 Discuss the following issue with your group. Many programs will post a vacant position so that staff members have an opportunity to apply for the opening before it is advertised to the general public. Will you do this in your program? Why or why not?

Job Descriptions

A job description "tells the employee what is expected and to some degree offers guidance on how to perform the job. It can be used to orient a new worker or in the ongoing supervision of an employee. Because the job description is a clear statement of duties, the employer can also use it to hold the employee accountable for performing the job satisfactorily" (Perreault 1988, 43). A written job description also helps you clarify the kind of person you are looking for and gives you a basis for screening applicants.

4.3 Your board decides that you need to recruit a new teacher for the toddler group. You also need to fill the cook's position. Write job descriptions for both including the following:

1. Job title
2. Requirements
    a. Educational
    b. Experiential

3. Job duties. List the primary duties and responsibilities they will be expected to carry out. Additional duties, such as evening meetings and written reports, should be specified.
4. Working conditions. These include working hours, breaks, meals, planning time.
5. Reporting relationships and limits of authority. To whom does this staff person report and under what circumstances must prior permission be sought?
6. Benefits such as health insurance, sick leave/personal days, vacation, paid holidays.

Recruiting

Next, contact agencies that might help you find qualified personnel. Some possible sources for teaching staff might be the following:

1. The placement office of a college or university near your center.
2. The state employment office in your community.
3. The local child care resource and referral agency or local chapter of NAEYC (National Association for the Education of Young Children) or ACEI (Association of Childhood Education International) might have a job bank that matches child care personnel with openings and/or advertises positions in their local or state publications. If you live in a small town or rural area, these organizations may not be near enough to help you.
4. If you have a good relationship with other center directors, you might ask them if they have applicants for whom they have no current openings. (This will have to be a reciprocal agreement, meaning you will have to share also. Be certain you have the applicant's permission before you release any information to another director.)
5. Make use of informal contacts in other community agencies. Ask parents if they know someone who might be interested.
6. Go through your substitute list to see if it contains good candidates.
7. Advertise the position.

4.4 Write a newspaper ad to be placed in the classified section for a teacher and/or assistant teacher. What information will you put in this ad? What materials will you ask the applicant to send? Be sure to set a deadline for receiving application materials.

Application Form

Often professional teaching jobs require applicants to submit a resume or curriculum vita and a letter of application. However, you may want to have a standard application form that everyone who seeks employment completes. Include educational background and a record of recent employment. Names and addresses of references who are familiar with the applicant's education and work experiences will be needed.

In all procedures it is important to follow the 1964 Civil Rights Act, which prohibits against discrimination in hiring practices. "The rule of thumb is that there must be a 'business necessity' for any question asked of the applicant. Some questions to avoid are date of birth or age, marital status, spouse's occupation, pregnancy issues and number of children, child-care arrangements, religious affiliation (although inquiry may be made as to whether the scheduled work days are suitable), membership in organizations (except those pertaining to the position), race or national origin (except for affirmative action information), arrest record (except as it pertains to child abuse), type of discharge from military, union memberships, and handicaps (only ask if person can perform job-specific functions). Inquiring about citizenship is not considered discriminatory; the administrator may ask to see a 1–151 Alien Registration Card or a 1–94 Arrival-Departure Card" (Decker and Decker 1988, 217). In some southwestern states all persons are required to sign a citizenship paper.

4.5   Design an application form for your program.

Screening Applicants

Your personnel committee and you, as the director, may have so many applicants for a position that you will want to narrow the number you will actually interview. You can set up a rating sheet that will list minimum qualifications. Those who have no formal training in early childhood education, for instance, could be eliminated from consideration.

If you have many who meet minimum requirements, you could rate each candidate in other ways. You could give points for years of training and/or experience. Then, the top scorers (however many you wish) could be invited for an interview.

Checking References

It is very important to check references. You can find out information that may help you decide whether a person works well with children and other adults. A reference can often be the deciding factor in choosing between two or more equally qualified applicants.

A reference form must be easy to complete or no one will bother with it. Using a checklist or rating scale works well. Leave room for written comments also. Some centers are very careful in how they word references because they do not want to be sued by former employees. Follow up by phone if you feel you need further information. Asking for three references that could be contacted by phone is an alternative to the reference form.

4.6   Design a reference form for a teaching position.

Send a letter to all applicants telling them that their applications have been received. Point out any other materials they need to send to complete the application. Give them a date when they can expect to hear from you.

Retain applications even if you can't use them right at the moment. If you have an opening at a later date, you can contact the applicant to see if she or he is still interested in a position with your center and would like to reapply.

Interviewing

Your hiring committee will want to have a list of written questions to ask all applicants. Having a standardized list means that all applicants are given similar consideration. These questions are simply a basis for getting a conversation going. It's a good idea to have seven or eight open-ended questions that explore the applicant's philosophy for working with young children, such as "How would you handle a situation where . . ." or "What would you do if . . ."

4.7 Write your interview questions for a teaching position. Exchange them with another group. Get their reactions. Then see if you want to make any changes.

Go over the job description with each candidate. Be certain they understand what would be expected of them. Elicit any questions they may have about the position.

As soon as your committee has interviewed a candidate, you will each rate that person using a rating sheet that is coordinated with your list of questions. It can be a checklist with "Does not meet, adequately meets, or excels in this qualification." Or, you might ask the committee to choose a number from one to five indicating how each one meets a specific criterion (one being "does not meet," five being "more than meets").

The interview process is very time consuming, but well worth it if it enables you to find the best people for the job.

Second Interviews

Before completing the hiring process invite the candidate to your center. Give the person a tour of the center. See how the applicant handles children and interacts with other adults. If you are having a difficult time deciding between two qualified candidates, have them each spend some time in an actual paid teaching situation for half a day. A second interview with you and the committee may also give you more information that will help you decide.

After you and the board members have made a decision about which applicant to hire, notify all the other applicants and thank them for applying. Write a letter to the successful applicant confirming employment. You might also tell applicants that their letters will be kept on file and that you will notify them of future openings for which they are qualified. Also send a notice to parents and staff members introducing the new employee. It is very important that parents do not arrive one morning to find that their child has a new teacher about whom they know nothing.

Some states require that a background check be done on all new employees in the child care field to screen out possible child abusers. Each person hired must submit information that is then processed through the criminal justice data banks.

With the current shortage of well-trained child care workers you may have trouble attracting the kind of staff members you want. Offering the best salaries you can afford, making the workplace and working conditions pleasant, hiring older workers and/or parents from your program, having a generous leave policy, and allowing job sharing are all suggestions for finding staff and keeping the turnover rate at a minimum (*Child Care Information Exchange* 1988). Paying for training or continuation of education is another incentive for staff members to remain. When hiring parents it works better for both parent and child if they are not in the same group.

Although salaries for child care workers have been abysmally low in the past and continue to be problematic in recruiting and keeping good staff (Whitebook, Howes, Phillips, and Pemberton 1989; Zinsser 1987), there is a growing awareness by the public that young children need quality care to develop optimally and that good care is expensive. Efforts to unionize child care employees, political lobbying by state and national organizations such as the National Association for the Education of Young Children (NAEYC) and the Children's Defense Fund, and the growing recognition of child care as a profession that deserves adequate compensation (NAEYC 1990) are beginning to have some impact on parents, legislators, and the general public. Until this is translated into an increased commitment to young children, more adequate funding of existing programs, and initiation of new publicly funded ways to help young families care for their children, it will still be a challenge to find and keep dedicated and talented child care workers.

Coordinating Staff Duties

Staffing Schedules

After you have figured out the number of children you will enroll, the hours of operation, and what activities will occur in the children's daily schedule, determine how many you will need on your teaching staff and what hours each staff member will work.

Check your state's requirements to determine age groups, maximum group size, and staff-to-child ratios for your program.

4.8 Decide how many teachers you will need for each age group in your program. Set up a daily teaching schedule for each group of children. Indicate which staff members will be licensed teachers, assistant teachers, and aides. Be certain you understand what the qualifications are in your state for each position. Some states require a fully qualified teacher for every so many children. Are there times of the day (early morning or late afternoon) when children from different age groups will be supervised together when numbers are small?

Orientation

Once you have hired a new staff member, you will need to spend time helping that staff member become a part of your center. Even though you will give each new staffer a copy of all pertinent policies to read, it is more meaningful to anyone new to the organization if you take time to talk over the program philosophy, purpose, and goals with them. Discussing emergency and accident procedures is imperative. Walking them through the emergency exit procedure and role-playing a medical emergency will help to avoid confusion if an accident or fire actually occurs. Going through the personnel policies step by step would also help the newcomer know more about how the program operates. The ethics of working with children and families should also be discussed (NAEYC 1989).

All this information would be overpowering in one session. A more effective approach might be to schedule an hour each week to spend with a new staff member during the first several weeks they are there. Since most employees will have a three- to six-month probationary period, you will also be discussing their job performance with them. This time also gives them a chance to ask you questions they have concerning the job. They will still be trying to figure out the limits and responsibilities of their position.

4.9 Make a list here of topics you would want to cover with each new staff member in the orientation process.

Substitutes

While continuity of care is one of the hallmarks of quality child care, it is normal that staff members must sometimes be absent. Finding and keeping good substitutes is often a problem for directors. In some centers other caregivers can stand in for the absent one for short periods. The director may have to take over a group occasionally. However, this solution doesn't work for anything but brief absences.

A teacher must be able to supervise the activities of several children at a time. *Photo by Steve Hermann*

Asking those applicants who are not hired if they would consider being placed on the sub list, calling in former employees who prefer to work part-time, and sharing subs with other centers are some ways to meet the need.

Substitutes also need to be given an orientation to the program and introduced to other teachers who could help in case of a problem. The teacher who will be gone can prepare in advance for a substitute by having a daily schedule posted, information about special needs certain children might have, and detailed plans for some "no fail" activities that children in the group enjoy. The director should also do a follow-up interview with each substitute to see how the day went and thank him or her for the help. Because the crisis in available trained child care workers is so great, good substitutes should be coddled. Those inexperienced substitutes who show an aptitude for working with children should be encouraged to apply for a more permanent position when one becomes available.

4.10 As the center director, what materials would you want to have available in the packet for substitutes? What would you ask each teacher to supply?

Summary

In this chapter you have carried out the steps a director will need to go through in hiring personnel to work in the program. The many parts to this process need to be executed with great prudence. Because of the intimate nature of the bond between caretaker and child, it is very important to find people who not only have some training and background in child development, but also are warm and accepting human beings and want to work with young children.

References

Child Care Information Exchange. 1988. On recruiting and selecting staff 60: 35–36.

Decker, C. A., and J. R. Decker. 1988. *Planning and administering early childhood programs.* Columbus, OH: Merrill.

National Association for the Education of Young Children. 1989. Code of ethical conduct. *Young Children* 45(1): 24–29.

National Association for the Education of Young Children. 1990. Position statement on guidelines for compensation of early childhood professionals. *Young Children* 46(1): 30–32.

Perreault, J. 1988. Developing your employee handbook: Job descriptions. *Child Care Information Exchange* 62: 43–46.

Rhode Island Department for Children and Their Families. 1984. *Day care centers and day nurseries: Standards for licensure.* Providence, RI.

Whitebook, M., C. Howes, D. Phillips, and C. Pemberton. 1989. Who cares? Child care teachers and the quality of care in America. (Research report). *Young Children* 45(1): 41–45.

Zinsser, C. 1990. The disgrace of child-care salaries. In *Issues and advocacy in early education* 28–29. ed. M. A. Jensen and Z. W. Chavalier. Boston: Allyn and Bacon.

4.1

Discuss who makes hiring and firing decisions in your program.

Write down different viewpoints. What was your group's final decision?

4.2

Will your center hire from within? Give reasons for and against this practice. What did your group decide?

4.3.a

Job description #1

Job title:

Educational requirements:

Experiential requirements:

Job duties:

Working conditions:

Reporting relationships:

Benefits:

4.3.b

Job description #2

Job title:

Educational requirements:

Experiential requirements:

Job duties:

Working conditions:

Reporting relationships:

Benefits:

4.4

Newspaper advertisement for a teacher and/or assistant teacher.

4.5

Application form for employment in your program.

4.6

Reference form for someone applying for a teaching position.

4.7

Interview questions for a teaching position.

1.

2.

3.

4.

5.

6.

7.

8.

9.

Reactions of another group.

4.8

Daily schedule for teaching staff.

4.9

The topics to be covered during orientation of new staff to the center.

1.

2.

3.

4.

5.

6.

7.

8.

4.10

Substitute teacher's packet.

List what materials you would want included.

1.

2.

3.

4.

5.

6.

7.

8.

5

SUPERVISION, EVALUATION, AND TRAINING OF STAFF

Chapter Outline

Staff management

Written records

Professional development

Summary

References

Assignments

5.1 List ways to use staff meetings to help in problem solving.

5.2 Discuss what your state requires for in-service training.

5.3 List ways to provide training for your staff.

5.4 Design a form to document your staff's training.

5.5 Develop a self-evaluation rating scale to be used by the teaching staff and the director.

5.6 Write personnel policies for your center.

5.7 Discuss confidentiality of personnel records.

5.8 Write a policy concerning confidentiality of personnel records.

5.9 Find early childhood professional organizations in your community.

5.10 Make decisions after examining the Code of Ethical Conduct.

5.11 Write a letter to legislators about a proposed bill.

Staff Management

Supervision, evaluation, and training of staff depends on building a good interpersonal relationship with each staff member. This is an ongoing process and will take much of the director's time and energy. The director should be available to talk when staff come in the morning or when they are leaving in the afternoon. Visiting classrooms, kitchen, and playgrounds and observing what is going on is a good way for her to gauge the abilities and training needs of the staff.

Staff members need to know that the director is supportive of their roles and realizes the demands of their jobs. The director should observe without interrupting or else schedule these visits when the staff member is likely to have time to talk. Albrecht (1991) suggested that directors take notes about what they are observing; these observations can then serve "... to pinpoint any problems and to identify any training or management needs" (21). She also suggested that the director have an agenda of things to look for, such as the way transitions are being handled, evidence of teamwork, or the kind of play behavior children are exhibiting. Another way is simply to make an anecdotal record of what you see without making any value judgments. The director can then use her notes as a basis for further communication with individual staff members. She can analyze her notes and talk to each teacher about what she saw when she visited his or her room. She might suggest some ways to overcome certain problems or suggest some readings or training opportunities that might help the teacher. Working with teachers by doing some occasional teaching or collaborating with them on a special project can help break down any barriers that exist.

Staff Meetings

Although a director will use many different methods of communicating with staff members (memos, newsletters, informal chats, one-on-one conferences), it is also necessary to establish a more formal way to communicate with the entire staff. The staff meeting makes discussion of issues and problems common to the center open to everyone. Each person gets an opportunity to speak and to listen to others. It is a good way to establish a sense of community and the feeling that all are working together to promote the center's goals. Legg (1991) felt that using icebreakers and get-acquainted games, or presenting humorous awards were good team-building experiences for starting meetings.

Finding a time when everyone can attend is always difficult. Most employees prefer that meetings be held during the work day. Sometimes it is possible to have a group of volunteers come at naptime once a month so that everyone can attend. However, some programs elect to hold evening meetings and give employees compensatory time off. Although it is most logical to have the meetings at the center, occasionally you could meet in someone's home, at a local restaurant, or even take a staff field trip (Legg 1991).

Having a regularly scheduled time to have staff meetings ensures that problems will be brought up before they escalate. You and your staff will need to work out how often meetings are to be held. Weekly meetings may be too often; monthly meetings may not be enough. Some agencies announce the schedule for the year so everyone knows when each meeting will be. Staff should be involved as much as possible in the planning and presenting of agenda items. Give everyone a copy of the agenda a few days in advance. Start meetings on time and stay within time limits. Decker and Decker (1988) suggested that minutes of the meeting be distributed to staff members and approved before sending them to the board of directors and/or filing them.

The director has the responsibility of preparing and distributing the agenda, making sure that all sides get heard, and keeping the meeting moving using parliamentary procedure. Sciarra and Dorsey (1990) warned against allowing staff meetings to deteriorate into gripe sessions. The administrator must help staff use this time constructively to discover ways to resolve some of the difficulties they encounter on the job. Often teachers and other staff members have insights into a situation that the director does not have. Staff meetings can be a time to examine many topics that are of interest to the whole staff. Discussing a particular child's needs, talking about ways to improve supervision on the playground, planning for in-service training or using meeting time to view a video or listen to a guest speaker, or reacting to the board's change of policy in the way staff are to be evaluated are some

Staff meetings are a time to solve problems and give each other support. *Photo by Steve Hermann*

examples of agenda items. If some topics are of interest or concern to only part of the staff, that group could meet separately.

5.1 Make a list of some ways staff meetings could be used to help solve some of the center's problems.

Beyond the staff meeting, there must be some way for staff members to communicate on a daily basis. Keeping a log of daily observations, which includes remarks such as "Child A is being picked up by her father before naptime" or "Child B complained that his ear hurt," is one way of letting the next shift know what is going on in that classroom. This same log can be used by parents to leave messages when they bring or pick up their child.

Written memos are a good way to convey routine information, but they are no substitute for the give and take of staff meetings.

Staff Training

Administrators of child care programs know that the quality of the program they are able to offer to children and their families depends to a large extent on the training of the teaching staff. Administrators will want to do everything they can to provide appropriate, ongoing in-service education to those involved with the children's program.

States vary considerably in their requirements for in-service training. In Hawaii (Department of Social Services and Housing 1982) the director is required to make available to all staff and volunteers information about any form of training available and to encourage staff growth and development. No formal requirement, however, is made of staff members.

Virginia requires eight hours of in-service training for teaching staff (Department of Social Services 1989). Texas (Department of Human Services) requires fifteen in-service hours for staff members and twenty for directors. Minnesota (Department of Human Services) requires teaching staff to hold current first aid and CPR (cardiopulmonary resuscitation) certificates and to spend a minimum of 2 percent of their annual work load in training. One quarter of the training must be from a resource outside the center. All training must be pertinent to the job and ages of children staff are serving.

The director should set up and supervise training for the staff. Some of the training geared to the whole staff could be based on the program evaluation (see chapter 13), the perceived needs of staff members themselves, and staff and parent evaluation instruments (Abbott-Shim 1990; Benham, Miller, and Kontos 1988). For example, if most of the teachers feel they need to know about "emergent literacy," an expert in early reading could be brought into the center for an evening or Saturday workshop. Much of the training, however, will need to be individually designed for each person and should be linked to his or her evaluation. For instance, if an assistant teacher has trouble with classroom management, a workshop on handling transitions sponsored by another center might be very appropriate for her to attend. Establishing a coherent plan for developing a professional development component for the entire program is also necessary. Wooden, Baptiste, and Reyes (1991) have outlined steps that have proven effective in establishing a programwide plan.

Hildebrand (1990) made suggestions about how to help staff improve performance and keep up-to-date through in-service training. She suggested using a positive approach when talking about the staff members' behaviors and traits, giving them choices, and helping them appreciate how improving their skills helps children. She also felt that soliciting staff suggestions for in-service education and bringing ideas back to share from the director's own training were good ways to interest them in getting more training.

Directors have a variety of resources available to assist them in planning in-service for their child care staff. Regional resource and referral agencies generally provide low-cost training. Local colleges or technical schools provide courses or workshops. Public libraries will supply books and videotapes. Often staff members can put on workshops for each other based on some special training or experiences they have had. Exchanging visits with teachers from other programs can be a learning experience for staff members. The director can also hire a consultant to provide some special expertise. Sometimes free or inexpensive training is available through community education programs or other social agencies. Abbott-Shim (1990) suggested that peer coaching is an effective way of helping new staff members incorporate training content into the classroom. Setting up a mentoring system will help beginners to learn necessary skills and will give a new dimension to the seasoned employee's job. Sometimes groups of centers collaborate to provide training. Local, state, and regional early childhood professional organizations put on annual conferences.

The director is responsible for seeing that training needs are identified and then working with the board to see that funds are available to support staff in their efforts to improve their skills. A national study of child care centers found the quality of care to be directly correlated to the training of the staff (Ruopp, Travers, Glantz, and Coelen 1979). The *Child Care Information Exchange* often has articles from directors with suggestions of field-tested training ideas.

The director also needs to follow up with each teacher to see that the training that has been provided is reflected in the actual practice with children (Wooden, Baptiste, and Reyes 1991).

5.2 Read your state regulations to see what in-service training your state requires for teaching staff.

5.3 Brainstorm and list some ways you, as a director, could provide in-service training for your staff.

5.4 Design a form to keep track of each staff member's in-service training. Include the topics that were covered, where and when the training was done, and who did the training.

Evaluating Staff

Evaluation of staff members is part of the director's job and can serve many purposes. It can be used to help you and the board decide if a person's employment will be continued, if they have areas that need to be improved, and if they will be considered for a raise or offered tenure. Whatever the purpose, evaluation should be based on your observations of staff performance. Your criteria for evaluation should be closely related to the job description under which each staff member was hired. Let the person you are evaluating know when you will be observing. If you are evaluating a teacher, spend an hour in the classroom. See what she or he has planned for the children to do that day. Discover how he or she relates to each child. Look at what kind of classroom management techniques the teacher uses.

Because each program is different, each one should develop criteria for evaluating staff members. Decker and Decker (1988) said, "Characteristics often evaluated are (1) physical characteristics—the physical health and vitality conducive to the effective performance of the position; (2) mental ability—the ability to conceptualize the philosophy of the program, the needs of the children and adults involved, and the employee's role and the roles of others as they relate to the position; (3) professional qualifications—knowledge of the methods and materials used in performing one's role; and (4) personal attributes—enthusiasm, poise, ability to adjust to frustrations, ability to cooperate with colleagues, and ability to accept constructive criticism" (231).

Some centers ask staff members to rate their own performances. This can help the teaching staff become aware of their strengths and weaknesses and gives them a feeling of involvement in the process. Johnson (1988) suggested that staff write performance statements that tell what they have done in several agreed-upon categories such as parent-teacher communication or daily planning. These statements simply tell what the person did and do not analyze why he or she chose to do something in a certain way. The director can use this self-assessment to talk to that staff member about how he or she perceives his or her abilities.

The director or evaluator will also observe the person noting practices that are beneficial for children and areas where improvement should be sought. The director will meet with the staff member and together they will make specific plans for improvement. This may include some in-service training. Usually, a time is set when some form of training must be completed and the staff member re-evaluated.

Although the administrator of a program will be doing informal observations and evaluations continually, this more formal evaluation will need to be done at least once or twice during the probation period. Seasoned staff members will need an annual evaluation. Even if their work is excellent, this is an opportunity to give them recognition for the good job they are doing. We all need to know that the job we are doing is appreciated.

Morris (1989) gathered suggestions from directors about ways they have found to increase respect for teachers. Beyond good pay, benefits, time off, appropriate supervision, and control in the classroom, there are many ways to increase each staff member's self-respect and respect for other staff, as well as parents' and the public's recognition for the important job child care workers do.

Writing about what individual teachers have accomplished in the parent newsletter, having a party to celebrate what staff have done together, giving praise and encouragement to each staff member, and giving recognition to staff in notices that go out to the public are some ways to help staff members see that they are valued.

5.5   Develop a self-evaluation form to be completed by individual teachers. Discuss how the director could use this instrument as a starting point for improving a staff member's skills.

Termination

Unfortunately, sometimes certain employees do not perform their job satisfactorily. As soon as you have misgivings about an employee's performance, call that person into your office, discuss your dissatisfaction with them, and work out steps that the person will have to take to improve. To avoid possible law suits should termination later be warranted, document any incidents that you consider infringements of that employee's job description, noting the date, time, place, causes, and results of questionable behavior.

After warnings have been issued and disciplinary measures tried, it may still be necessary to dismiss an employee. Of course, when an employee threatens or hurts a child or presents a danger to self or others, immediate dismissal and/or contact of legal authorities is necessary.

The following might be some possible reasons for terminating a staff member. (This list is a *modification* of "Notification of Intent Not to Rehire" found in Cherry, Harkness, and Kuzma 1987, 145.)

1. Ineffective because of personal or family problems.
2. Has another job or responsibilities that leave no energy for this job.
3. Doesn't get along well with other staff members.
4. Has been evaluated and found to have poor skills for working with children.
5. Does not respect the confidentiality of information regarding parents, children, or other staff members. Gossip can be damaging.
6. Has given erroneous information in the application process.
7. Has been insubordinate to director/supervisor and has refused to carry out a reasonable request.
8. Discourteous to others.
9. Has a physical or mental disability that makes it difficult to carry out responsibilities.
10. Has difficulty communicating with parents.
11. Is addicted to alcohol or narcotics.
12. Has been convicted of a felony or misdemeanor involving a morals charge.
13. Is absent too often to be an effective staff member.
14. Is consistently late.
15. Is negligent in supervising children.
16. Shows favoritism to certain children or has accepted a gratuity to give special treatment to a child or another employee.
17. Is unhappy in the job and reluctant to continue employment.

Supervising Staff

It is essential to the well-being of your program that you establish and retain good rapport with all staff members. Even when conflicts and differences of opinion occur, as they inevitably will, directors must maintain professionalism in interacting with all staff members. You also do not want your personal friendships with certain staff members to impinge on your administrative decision making. You want to win the cooperation of staff members, but, ultimately, you are still in charge of running the program.

Gould (1990) emphasized that directors must do all they can to get decent salaries for their staff members. A national study found that the most important predictor of the quality of care children receive, among the adult work environment variables, is staff wages (Howes, Pemberton, Phillips, and Whitebook 1989). Directors must also give new staff members a good orientation so they understand the philosophy of the program and are clear about their specific responsibilities.

Kohl (1989) stressed that the child care center must be a place where the needs of both adults and children are observed and met. The director is the key to organizing and promoting activities that will encourage a positive atmosphere and relationships. Honoring staff members on their birthdays with cards, a gift, the day off or involving teachers in goal setting and curriculum development are some simple ways to keep morale high.

Everyone needs recognition and affirmation. Show approval of your staff members. Be interested in what they are doing. Though you must be equitable in your dealings with each of them, you also must recognize that everyone is an individual with different abilities and talents. You want to help each to develop professionally. You can also serve as a model of the kind of behavior and expectations you have for each one of them.

Use encouragement. Sciarra and Dorsey (1990) pointed out that "Just as the classroom teacher makes sure that encouragement is specific, is focused on process, is usually given in private, and is neither judgmental nor evaluative, so the director keeps these same principles in mind when working with staff" (6). Saying to a teacher in a preschool class "I like the way you took time to explain to Josh that carrying blocks over his head might be dangerous" is more specific than saying "You handled that well."

Be prepared to mediate conflicts between staff members. Often they want the same thing; they just have different ways of getting there. Help each one to see that in child care, as in many other endeavors, many different methods can be effective. Hearing both sides of an argument and helping staff come to some workable solutions can be helpful in maintaining morale. "Offering to sit down and chat with everyone involved ..." is a good strategy to use in defusing conflicts (Gould 1990, 6).

Be an advocate for your staff. See that the board is generous in its leave and vacation policies. Because child care is an intensive and emotionally draining profession and the dropout rate is high, see that staff have adequate breaks, take an occasional mental health day, and have enough vacation time to find renewal. Some programs structure the teaching staff's time so that each worker has some planning time or other time away from children during the day.

Finding and resolving other stress-causing factors such as overcrowding, insufficient materials, or absenteeism is the job of the director. Ultimately, it is the administrator's job to make it easier for the rest of the staff to do their jobs. Whenever you can resolve a problem that might escalate into stress for the teacher or cook, you are facilitating the smoother running of the program and freeing the staff to do the job for which they were hired.

Listen to staff members. Consider their suggestions when planning for the program. Be available when they want to vent their feelings. "I can guarantee that if you can muster the nerve to get engaged in a discussion of the 'little things' that rule the lives in your organization, it will reveal the strategic stumbling blocks to higher quality, and more responsiveness" (Gould 1990, 6). Allowing free expression of emotions can be therapeutic. This means you can be very helpful to individual staff members by playing the counseling role.

Supporting your staff members in dealing with parents and board members is another way of confirming their worth. Let staff know that the job they are doing is important and that they are valued members. It is helpful to review your purposes, goals, and philosophy with staff members fairly often to make certain everyone sees the reasons that you all need to work together.

Written Records

Personnel Policies

Personnel policies include all information about the terms of employment, job responsibilities, and the rights of employees. Having written policies saves confusion and discussion and ensures fairness for both employee and employer. Written policies also save time for employers because established procedures can be followed. They also let staff know what is expected of them and reduce anxiety and insecurity.

Sciarra and Dorsey (1990) have an excellent example of a well-formulated personnel policy, which may be consulted *after* you have had an opportunity to construct one for your center.

5.6 Write personnel policies for your program. At a minimum you will want to include the following in the personnel policies:

1. A statement of the purpose, goals, and philosophy of the program.
2. How the personnel policies are established for the program. Include a process for frequent review of policies. Also describe how policies can be amended or changed.
3. Terms of employment
   a. Describe what positions your program will have.
   b. Define what is meant by probationary, temporary, permanent, full-time, part-time, or any other terms used to describe the job.
   c. Include a nondiscrimination clause.
   d. Describe how vacancies will be filled through the hiring procedure. Include a clear statement of who has the authority to hire and terminate staff.
   e. Describe how staff members may change positions, resign, or retire.
4. Job description
   a. Briefly outline the qualifications and duties of each staff position.
   b. Health requirements for staff (consult your state licensing regulations).
   c. Hours of employment and method of clocking in and out.
   d. When salaries will be paid.
   e. Staff conduct. This may include dress code, smoking, and eating regulations. (The staff are often required to eat lunch with the children. Most child care centers allow no smoking on the premises.)
5. Salaries and fringe benefits
   a. How salaries are determined.
   b. Process for reviewing salaries and recommending increases.
   c. How compensatory time may be accrued and how it may be used.
   d. Fringe benefits. These may include vacation pay, holiday pay, sick leave, and hospitalization or health care benefits.
6. Attendance and leave
   a. Expectations for attendance. How tardiness will be handled. What notification employees must give if they will be absent. What will happen if absenteeism is excessive.
   b. Vacation. How length of employment affects days of vacation. How requests for vacation dates will be processed.
   c. Sick and/or personal leave. How much time will be granted. When a physician's statement is required.
   d. Jury duty. How salary will be continued. How jury pay will affect salary.
   e. Paid legal holidays.
7. Disciplinary action and methods of appeal
   a. Procedure for warnings, suspension, and terminations
   b. How disciplinary actions may be appealed (usually there is a definite time limit). A grievance process should be outlined giving the hierarchy of command.
   c. Termination of service. Reasons for dismissal. Written notice of dismissal. Termination interviews. Provision for immediate termination or a notice period. Termination of benefits.
8. Evaluation. How and when evaluations will be done. How promotions are determined.
9. In-service training requirements. Documentation that requirements are met. (Many states require first aid and CPR training and updating.)

10. Personnel records. This will list the contents of the file to be maintained for each staff member and who will have access to it. (Written permission of the staff member is required before records can be read by anyone other than the staff member, the director or supervisor, or the state licensing agent.)

Personnel Records

For each staff member you will need to keep a file of materials that should include the following:

1. The staff person's name, home address, home telephone number, and date of birth.
2. The telephone number of a person to be notified in an emergency.
3. The staff person's job description.
4. The staff person's application, resume, and documentation that the person meets the education and experience requirements specified.
5. Documentation that the staff person has completed the orientation to the program.
6. Documentation (for teaching staff) that the staff person has completed first aid and CPR training (if required).
7. Documentation of completion of in-service training. This should include training topic, source of training, number of hours completed, and method used to document mastery of the subject.
8. Documentation of procedures for and completion of an annual evaluation of the staff person's work and specification of in-service training needs.
9. Documentation of any disciplinary action, including termination.
10. Insurance forms (if involved in group insurance).
11. Health records.
12. Service records. This may include date of present employment, level/age of children cared for, absences incurred, leaves taken, salary received, date of termination of employment.
13. Documentation that the staff person has completed the applicant background study (if required).

5.7 In your group discuss how confidentiality of these records will be maintained.

5.8 Write a policy statement concerning confidentiality that will be included in your center's personnel policies.

Professional Development

Early Childhood Professional Organizations

Membership in a professional association can bring many rewards. Every person with a career that involves young children and their families can belong to an organization that serves their needs and interests. Through their journals and other publications, conferences, and reviews of research organizations help their memberships keep current in the field. They also offer opportunities for meeting and discussing issues with other professionals. They can support lobbying efforts, sponsor research and public awareness campaigns, and be major advocates for the profession. Joining a professional organization helps early childhood educators wield more influence than might be possible for just one individual.

Participating in organizations can also bring recognition to your program. Whenever you or one of your teachers makes a presentation at a conference or serves in a leadership position, that lets people know that your center is concerned about keeping up-to-date and providing valuable service to the community.

5.9 Appendix B contains a list of professional organizations that are concerned with young children. Check to see if any of them have chapters in your community or region. List those that do.

A Code of Ethics

One of the marks of a profession is that it has a Code of Ethics that governs the behavior of its members. The National Association for the Education of Young Children (1989) has prepared a Code of Ethical Conduct (see Appendix C) that monitors how early childhood professionals interact with children, parents, colleagues, and the larger community.

5.10 Child care center directors must make many difficult decisions. Right and wrong are not always apparent. Read the Code of Ethical Conduct (Appendix C) to help make decisions about what actions you will take. What ideal(s) or principle(s) best applies to the following situations?

1. A parent brings her three-year-old, who is hearing impaired, to your program. The school district's special education team has recommended that the child be integrated into a regular child care center. Board members object to your admitting her because of the extra work it will be for the staff.

2. The teacher in the toddler group brings a little boy to you. His legs and back have bruises and scars. You have noticed that this child seems afraid of adults.

3. A parent comes to you and tells you confidentially that she found that her child has lice. She's willing to treat her child, but she doesn't want anyone else to know about it.

4. The board has a policy that there can be no smoking at the center. However, you have smelled cigarette smoke in the restroom and suspect that some employees are smoking there on their breaks.

5. You have been asked to give a reference for a teacher whom you fired for leaving children unattended on the playground.

Advocacy

Children do not vote, which is one reason their welfare and rights are not given priority by politicians. Directors and teachers of young children can be leaders in advocating for legislation that is beneficial for families. Educating parents about their rights, organizing a letter-writing campaign to state legislators, attending city council or school board meetings, or testifying before a state committee about the needs of the children in your community are all examples of ways to be involved in improving life for children.

Find out what children need. Read the literature and speak to experts. Then see how children in similar circumstances are being helped. If possible, join forces with others in the same struggle. Get parents involved. Determine what strategies will be used to reach the desired goals. Communicate exactly what you want to those who have the power to make changes. Follow up to see that promised actions are taken and that those who helped are given thanks and recognition.

5.11   Find out about current legislation that is being proposed in your local government, the state legislature, or the U.S. Congress that will have an impact on young children or families. Choose one bill. Find out all you can about it. What position has been taken by your representative? Write a letter to a legislator stating your reasons for supporting the bill or state your objections to it. Be brief, but make certain that you get your points across. Read your draft to members of your group. Get their suggestions for improving the wording. Submit an original and one copy along with an addressed and stamped envelope to the instructor. Your letter will be mailed and the copy returned to you.

Summary

Managing a staff and supervising their activities is one of the principal duties of a director. Setting up staff meetings, observing and evaluating staff, and helping staff get in-service training are the responsibilities of the program administrator. Proposing personnel policies to the board, keeping personnel records, and being involved in the hiring and firing of staff are also requirements of the job. Finding time to get involved in local and national children's organizations, adhering to a code of ethics, and taking part in child advocacy efforts can add to the director's own professional development.

References

Abbott-Shim, M. S. 1990. In-service training: A means to quality care. *Young Children* 45(2): 14–18.

Albrecht, K. 1991. Managing teacher performance while walking around. *Child Care Information Exchange* 78: 21–22.

Benham, N., T. Miller, and S. Kontos. 1988. Pinpointing staff training needs in child care centers. *Young Children* 43(4): 9–16.

Cherry, C., B. Harkness, and K. Kuzma. 1987. *Nursery school and day care management guide.* 2d ed. Belmont, CA: Fearon.

Decker, C. A., and J. R. Decker. 1988. *Planning and administering early childhood programs.* 4th ed. Columbus, OH: Merrill.

Gould, N. P. 1990. Work commitment and job satisfaction for program staff: How to build it. *Day Care and Early Education* 17: 4–7.

Hawaii Department of Social Services and Housing. 1982. *Licensing of group day care centers and group day care homes.* Honolulu, HI.

Hildebrand, V. 1990. *Management of child development centers.* 2d ed. New York: Macmillan.

Howes, C., C. Pemberton, D. Phillips, and M. Whitebook. 1989. Who cares? Child care teachers and the quality of care in America. *Young Children* 45: 41–45.

Johnson, J. M. 1988. A performance based approach to staff evaluation. *Child Care Information Exchange* 62: 10–13.

Kohl, D. M. 1989. Supervisory techniques for positive performance. *Day Care and Early Education* 17(1): 16–18.

Legg, J. 1991. Successful staff meetings. *Child Care Information Exchange* 77: 52–53.

Morris, S. 1989. Recognition for a job well done: Increasing respect for teachers. *Child Care Information Exchange* 69: 15–17.

National Association for the Education of Young Children. 1989. Code of ethical conduct. *Young Children* 45(1): 25–29.

Ruopp. R., J. Travers, F. Glantz, and C. Coelen. 1979. *Children at the center. Final report of the National Day Care Study (Vol. 1).* Cambridge, MA: Abt Associates.

Sciarra, C. J., and A. G. Dorsey. 1990. *Developing and administering a child care center.* 2d ed. Albany: Delmar.

Virginia Department of Social Services. 1989. *Minimum standards for licensed child care centers.* Roanoke, VA: Department of Human Services.

Wooden, S. L., N. Baptiste, and L. Reyes. 1991. Required: A professional development component for every early childhood education program. *Day Care and Early Education* 18(3): 26–27.

5.1

Staff meetings.

List some ways staff meetings could be used to solve center problems.

1.

2.

3.

4.

5.

6.

7.

8.

5.2

Requirements for in-service training for teaching staff in your state.

5.3

Brainstorm ideas for ways to provide in-service training for your staff.

1.

2.

3.

4.

5.

6.

7.

8.

5.4

Prepare a form for documenting staff training. Include topics covered, where and when it was done, and who did the training.

5.5

Develop a self-evaluation form for teachers. What topics will you include?

5.6

Personnel policies for your child care program.

5.7

Confidentiality of personnel records.

What measures will you take to protect staff records?

5.8

Write a policy statement concerning confidentiality of staff records.

5.9

Early childhood professional organizations.

List those available to you in your community or region.

Code of ethics.

Write down your answers to the questions asked in this section. Find the appropriate "Ideal" or "Principle" that would guide your response.

Question 1

Question 2

Question 3

Question 4

Question 5

5.11

Advocacy.

Write the rough draft of a letter to a legislator stating why you support or oppose legislation that has been proposed.

6

FINANCIAL AND LEGAL CONSIDERATIONS

Chapter Outline

Building and equipping the center

Managing finances

Legal requirements

Summary

References

Assignments

6.1 Write a purchase list of furnishings for a classroom and three pieces of playground equipment.

6.2 Total the costs and answer questions.

6.3 Make an annual budget proposal for your center.

6.4 Estimate your income based on tuition and other sources.

6.5 Adjust your budget.

6.6 Write a grant proposal for your program.

6.7 Revise your annual budget again with 30 percent gained from grants.

6.8 Discuss insurance coverage needed by child care centers.

6.9 Discuss fiscal and legal matters with a center director.

Building and Equipping the Center

Start-Up Costs

Starting a new center from scratch can involve large amounts of money. Some of the expenses will be costs of land and construction for building a new center or for renovating an existing structure; buying kitchen, office, maintenance, and classroom equipment and furniture; connecting utilities; insurance; licensing fees; purchasing program materials; and paying salaries, orientation, and training costs for staff. This money may come from investors or may be arranged through loan agreements. It is important to remember that the center will not operate to capacity right away. Therefore, it is necessary to have enough cash on hand to meet all expenses during the first few months when you will be paying out more than you take in.

Furnishing A Classroom

6.1 To get some idea of how much money you will need, you will make up a purchase list of all the things you will need to set up one infant, toddler, or preschool classroom. Use current catalogs from educational suppliers. Your instructor may have a limit on how much you can spend on one room.

Generally, state regulations say that child care centers must have adequate and appropriate furnishings and materials for children's use. Because the furnishings you buy will be used for many years by a large number of children, it is important to find sturdy, well-made toys and equipment. Quality products are always expensive, but worth it if they last a long time and serve the purposes intended. Consult with the teachers to see what they want in their rooms. A piece of furniture or an educational game that is never used can be an expensive mistake to be avoided.

Utah has a list of suggested materials (see Appendix D). Minnesota has minimum equipment and materials lists for each age group—infants, toddlers, preschoolers, and school-age. The following list will help you if you chose to equip a preschool classroom (Minnesota DHS 1989, 20–25):

- A. Furnishings:
    1. one area rug or carpet per group;
    2. one nonfolding child size chair per child;
    3. one cot or bed and waterproof mattress per child (mats are acceptable for programs operating during the day for less than five hours). This subitem is not required for preschoolers in programs operating for less than five hours per day if rest is not indicated as part of the center's child care program;
    4. two square feet of wall or bulletin board display space per child (one-half at child's eye level);
    5. one partially enclosed space equipped for quiet activity per group;
    6. one linear foot of open shelving per child; and
    7. 20 linear inches of child size table edge per child.
- B. Program equipment and materials:
    1. arts and crafts supplies, such as clay or playdough, tempera or fingerpaints, white or colored paper, paste, collage materials, paint brushes, washable felt type markers, crayons, scissors, and smocks;
    2. two books per child;
    3. 48 large building blocks per group;
    4. 200 small building blocks per group;

5. five pieces of dramatic play equipment or sets of Montessori Practical Life equipment per group;
6. materials and accessories required for subitem (5) to carry out the theme of the activity;
7. one double easel per group;
8. three pieces of durable, indoor, large muscle equipment per group;
9. three pieces of durable, outdoor, large muscle equipment per group;
10. one mirror, at least 12 inches by 36 inches, made of Plexiglas or a similar plastic or safety glass, per group;
11. one music source such as a tape recorder or record player per group and music selections appropriate for the source;
12. one set of cognitive developmental equipment and materials, such as puzzles and number and letter games, per child;
13. two sets of manipulative equipment, such as interlocking plastic forms, per child;
14. one rhythm instrument per child.

C. Supplies
1. an adequate amount of facial tissue;
2. an adequate amount of single service towels;
3. an adequate amount of liquid hand soap.

3.2 Add up the total to see how much it would cost to furnish one room and buy three pieces of outdoor equipment. Then answer the following questions:

1. What did you learn from this exercise?
2. Where might you look to find some bargains to keep costs down?
3. What different items would you need for an infant program? a toddler program? a school-age program?

Managing Finances

The Operating Budget

You have already made many decisions that will affect the budget for your particular program. The number and ages of the children you will serve, the community in which your program is located, the teacher-child ratios, the general economic climate, and the kinds of services you offer will also be factors to consider when planning your budget.

Assuming that you have found the money to set up your program, you are now ready to prepare an operating budget. Usually the director will work with the Finance Committee of the board to propose an annual operating budget. The board will listen to the presentation, make any revisions they deem necessary, and then approve a budget for a full fiscal year.

An operating budget differs from a start-up budget in that it assumes that renovation/building costs and purchases of major equipment have already been made. Planning an operating budget is a process that has many steps. The first budget your group makes will look at some crude estimates (guesses really) of what you want in your program and how much each item will cost.

3.3 Use the following outline to guide you in making an annual budget proposal for your program.

These sturdy blocks enable children to build impressive structures. Though expensive, they should last many years. *Photo by Steve Hermann*

    I.   Administration
- A. Salaries
  1. Director
  2. Secretary or other office staff
  3. FICA, SDI, and other personnel taxes. This varies with the amount of benefits, such as hospitalization, that the employer pays. For the purposes of this budget, estimate this at 23%.
  4. Substitutes (for sick leave, vacations, etc.)
- B. Office supplies
- C. Administrative equipment
- D. Other administrative costs (licensing fee, printing costs, advertising, postage, telephone, bookkeeper/accountant's fees)

    II.   Program
- A. Salaries
  1. Teachers and child care assistants or aides
  2. All salary expenses as above
  3. Substitute teachers or other staff members
- B. Program supplies
- C. Program equipment (new and replacement)
- D. In-service training costs, conference fees, journals, etc. (Sometimes each employee is given a maximum dollar amount to pay training costs. The training money can be distributed equally or be based on amount of time the employee has been working in the center.)

III. Supplemental services
   A. Food and kitchen supplies. Put this in your budget even if it is reimbursed by the USDA (United States Department of Agriculture). If reimbursed, put the figure in parentheses and do not count it in your total.
   B. Cook's salary. Again, put in parentheses the part of the cook's salary that is reimbursed.
   C. Pets and supplies
   D. Parent education
   E. Insurance, scholarships, and other charges unique to your program.
   F. Transportation
   G. Medical (first aid) supplies
IV. Plant operation
   A. Rent or mortgage
   B. Custodian/Matron salaries
   C. Utilities
   D. Cleaning equipment and supplies
   E. Maintenance and repair of grounds and equipment
   F. Other

Personnel costs will constitute the major share of your expenditures. The National Day Care Study (Ruopp, Travers, Glantz, and Coelen 1979) found that on the average the budgets of child care centers expended 69 percent on personnel costs, 10 percent on rent or building costs, 16 percent on equipment and supplies, and 5 percent to other operating costs. Hildebrand (1990) suggested that with the emphasis on adequate salaries for child care workers in the past decade, personnel costs may have risen in proportion to other costs.

Centers that operate "for profit" would expect to make a margin of at least 15 percent over expenditures in order to pay dividends to investors. Private profit-making corporations make up an increasingly large share of the child care market (Neugebauer 1988).

Income

Now that you have some idea of what your costs will be, you will look at what to expect in the way of income. The largest source of income will be the tuition that parents pay for their child to attend. Because the staff costs for infants and toddlers is higher than for preschoolers or school-age children, parents of younger children are usually charged more. Your group or your instructor will survey local child care programs to determine the current average rates charged. Add together all the income from tuition. Figure an attendance rate of fifty weeks per year at about 85 percent capacity (unless your group has chosen to operate a program that meets on a less-than-year-round basis).

5.4 Determine what your income will be.

   1. What will your income be from tuition?
   2. What other income will you have?
   3. What is your total income?

5.5 Now go back and make some adjustments in your budget based on what income you will have available.

Financial and Legal Considerations

Directors conduct much of the center's business over the phone. *Photo by Steve Hermann*

Making Purchases

Once the board approves the budget, the director is at liberty to spend the money appropriated for each line item. It is your job to see that the money lasts until the end of the fiscal year and that you do not overspend in any one area. However, sometimes unexpected events may cause expenses for which you have not planned. For instance, the furnace may break down and require repairs that exceed the amount budgeted. You must then get board approval to shift funds from another line item to the repair budget to cover this expense.

The board may also require you to get estimates before you buy anything that costs over a certain amount. If you are planning to purchase a new stove for the kitchen and a changing table for the infant classroom, you would write up the specifications for what you want and send it to three or four suppliers and ask them to submit bids. You and the board will come to an agreement about which supplier offers the best item at the most reasonable price before signing a purchase agreement. The following are two examples of "specs."

Kitchen Stove. Electric, four-burner, self-cleaning oven with glass door, all controls on top back panel (out of reach of small children), width—thirty inches. Drawer under oven for pans.

Changing Table. Solid hardwood frame, 36" H × 40" L × 20" deep, with three adjustable shelves, six plastic tote boxes.

Here are some tips for making purchases within the budget.

1. Keep current catalogs and price lists.
2. Make a list of vendors you have found reliable.
3. Think about buying in quantity. Often items cost less if bought in bulk. This is only possible, however, if you have room to store the materials and they will not deteriorate with time.
4. Be aware of shipping costs and the time it takes to get an order. Morris (1990) has suggested that checking for damages and following the return policy carefully can help ensure satisfaction.
5. Protect your credit rating by paying your bills on time (Sackett, 1990).
6. The best time to order from educational supply houses is early in the year. The worst time is between July 1 and September 15 (Sackett 1990).

Raising Money

Most nonprofit day care centers have a difficult time managing on the income from tuition alone. Programs have tried all kinds of ingenious schemes for supplementing their budgets. Bake sales, carnivals, thrift shops, and spaghetti dinners are all fun, promote public relations, and get staff and parents working together. They are important to do for these reasons. However, they are also very labor intensive and do not bring much return for the amount of work that is put into them.

Organizing an annual giving campaign can be a good way to raise money. Scallan (1987) has identified eight essential points for managing a successful fund drive. These are (1) know why you are raising the money, (2) set a financial goal, (3) target the message (parents of current and former students head the donor list), (4) tailor the appeal to the potential donor, (5) draft the letter, (6) cultivate donor response, (7) implement donor response, and (8) track and evaluate the campaign. It may be helpful in planning a fund drive to consider Scallan's (1987) observation: "Since 1985, individuals have been contributing 90 percent of all private, philanthropic dollars in the United States. Corporations give less than 10 percent of the total charitable giving" (9).

Grant Proposals

To bring in the money needed to sustain and build your program you will need to learn the skills necessary for writing successful grant proposals. This is a time-consuming, often-tedious task. However, it can garner funds that will allow you to expand the number of children you can care for or to improve the services you currently offer to families.

Although the probability of a small, nonprofit agency's attaining grants is low, child care organizations appear to do better than average when it comes to getting outside support. Improving child care options for families is a top priority in nearly every community in the nation.

Many steps are necessary to prepare a successful grant proposal. First, you must do research. Find out what kind of funding is available. What is being done in agencies similar to yours? What kinds of proposals are being funded? For instance, if everyone is interested in augmenting the number of infants served, you might make that the focus of your proposal. If computers are the "in" thing, show how your program would benefit by having one. If the prevention of child abuse is being funded, start a parent education program at your center.

To get this information, go talk to people. Visit other centers and talk to directors about "who is funding what." If feasible, link up with others to share information about fund-raising possibilities. Look for foundations who traditionally fund human service programs. Go to the public library and ask for a foundation directory. Ask the librarian for help in locating books and journals that tell what foundations are funding. Send for information and funding guidelines. Again, get names of whom to contact in each organization.

Although doing research on a national or regional level can put you in touch with the big foundations, do not neglect local sources. Go to businesses in your community. Find out who in the organization has anything to do with funding and make an appointment. Often they have funds earmarked for public service. Ask them for funding guidelines. Give them an education about your program or have a fact sheet ready that tells them a little of the history of your program and what it does. Even if they cannot fund you in the amount you need, they can often be a remarkable source of expertise or of "in-kind" service. For instance, they may lend you an executive to help you set up personnel policies or a bookkeeping plan, have their architect design a playground for you, offer to do your printing for you, or give you their used office machines. It is also very good public relations for them to be seen helping with local child care efforts.

Go to different sources for different items. Start-up costs can be divided into many different areas—building costs, equipment needs, landscaping, educational materials, playground resurfacing, and so on.

Go to meetings of public funders. Ask questions and get the information you need. Foundations and government agencies often hold proposal-writing seminars or workshops. Attend these. Local NAEYC chapters or resource and referral agencies also may have up-to-date information on current national or community grant opportunities.

Your local United Way, church groups, or other social agencies may be willing to fund you once you establish your nonprofit status. Find out when their next funding cycle starts and have your proposal ready to meet their deadlines.

Writing the proposal comes next. Some foundations have a certain form you must follow. Most will contain the following elements:

1. *The cover letter.* This is actually written last. It clearly summarizes your proposal. It tells how much money is being requested and how the money will be used. It gives the name, address, and phone number of the person to contact. You may want to include a few letters of endorsement in an appendix also.

2. *The introduction.* This narrative gives a brief history of your program, the qualifications of the staff, the governing board (a list of members names and addresses are attached in the appendix), and any other pertinent information about your program.

3. *Problem statement/needs assessment.* Define the needs you are trying to meet. Show that the children, the parents, or the community has the need. Discuss how the need could be met or the problem solved by having the proposed funding. Some funding sources are impressed by the uniqueness of the requests or of the program. What is special about your program or about what you are trying to do?

4. *Objectives.* Describe the ends you want to reach in measurable terms. This establishes the benefits of the funding.

5. *Methods.* Describe the activities to be employed to achieve the desired results.

6. *Evaluation.* Present a plan for determining the degree to which objectives are met and methods are followed. Evaluation criteria must be geared to the rest of the proposal. Did you do what you said you would? Were the ends actually achieved? Did you come closer to goals?

7. *Future funding.* Describe a plan for continuation beyond the grant period or the availability of other resources necessary to implement the grant. Where will future funding come from?

8. *Budget.* This is an itemized account of how the grant money will be spent. Make sure that this amount is the same everywhere in the proposal. This clearly states what funds are to be supplied by the funding source and which by the applicant or other parties. The funder may ask to see a copy of your entire budget. This can be added to the appendix.

9. *Appendix.* All supplemental materials pertinent to your proposal can be included here (e.g., letters of reference, list of board members, etc.).

Once you have sent the proposal, keep in contact with the foundation. If you are turned down, find out why. Maybe it is something that can be corrected in your next proposal. You have probably made some important contacts while working on this proposal. Perhaps they will be able to help you in the future. As disappointing as it may be, do not be discouraged. If your proposal fails to get funded from one source, revamp it and send it to another foundation.

6.6 Write a grant proposal for your center. First focus on a need that you anticipate. For this proposal, the maximum amount you may request is $5,000.

6.7 Assume that you have been successful in raising outside funds for your program, thus raising your annual income by 30 percent. Go back and revise your operating budget to reflect that increase. Instead of just increasing every item by the same percentage, really think about where you want to put the increased revenue.

Bookkeeping

Keeping track of the money that the center takes in and the amount it disperses is an essential part of the director's job.

An accountant who is familiar with the kind of reporting and tax information that you must have should set up the books for you. You may be able to get help from such agencies as the Service Corporation of Retired Executives (SCORE) or the Small Business Institute in your community. Or the accounting firm that you engage may come in and set up your books for you.

Office personnel can be trained to record all tuition transactions and keep track of staff members' hours. This information is then sent to the accountant who makes out payroll checks and prepares a monthly financial report. The accounting firm also prepares the center's quarterly income tax (IRS) and social security (FICA) reports.

If food services are underwritten by the USDA, office staff can also count the number of children present and number of meals served each day. These reports must be submitted to the government on a monthly basis.

Click and Click (1990) have found several IBM-compatible programs written especially for preschool administrators that could be helpful in budgeting, correspondence, recordkeeping, and other routine office procedures. They found that most older personal computers could handle the work and that the software was relatively inexpensive. Each piece of software does several different tasks and each has its strengths and weaknesses. These researchers claim that anyone who can operate an electric typewriter can master a computer. The software programs designed "just for preschools" all have a preprogrammed format and would be fairly easy to use.

Legal Requirements ✱

Certain things must be done if you are running any kind of business. Operating a day care center or other type or children's program is no exception. Below are listed some of the mandatory and/or recommended legal practices that should be used by child care centers (Kotin, Crabtree, and Aikman 1981).

1. *Employer identification number.* Getting an employer identification number from the IRS as soon as you set up the program is the first order of business. It is not necessary to have employees or to be operating yet. This rule applies whether you are a sole proprietor, a partner, or have set up a corporation.

2. *State unemployment insurance.* You must also participate in your state's unemployment insurance. In some states you pay a certain percentage of your center's total wages. In others you pay the actual costs when your former employees go on unemployment.

3. *Social Security payments.* In addition to taking Social Security payments out of the employee's wages, businesses also contribute a certain percentage. These must be deposited quarterly.

4. *Withholding exemption certificates.* Each new employee must fill out withholding exemption certificates (IRS-W-4 forms). As the employer, you must send out W-2 forms with the employee's annual earnings and taxes withheld by the end of January each year.

5. *Periodic tax returns.* Periodic tax returns must be filed quarterly. This varies depending on the dates of your fiscal year. Always file on time even if you can't pay as there are stiff penalties for late filing.

6. *Annual tax returns.* The annual tax return must be filed four months and fifteen days after the end of your fiscal year.

7. *Separate bank accounts.* A separate bank account is a must for corporations and a good idea for anyone operating a child care center. You must file with the bank the signatures of those who are authorized to write checks. Generally these checks should have two signatures—usually those of the director and a board officer.

8. *Written personnel policies and job descriptions.* These both help to keep employer/employee relations amicable and lessen conflict.

9. *An independent audit.* An independent annual audit is required of corporations who take in more than a certain amount. You need to contract with a Certified Public Accountant (CPA) firm in advance and see what it requires in the way of information. A letter of engagement is necessary. For most child care programs this would not be required. However, it is a good idea to have someone not employed by the center look over the books each year. Some agencies may do a formal audit every few years. If you are handling government funds, the government may require a yearly audit. Most states require an informational report giving the current membership of the board of directors and the sources of your center's income.

10. *Insurance needs.* General liability insurance, insurance on any vehicle used to transport children, workmen's compensation, and fire and theft insurance are all needed in the operation of a child care center (Child Care Law Center 1985). Fidelity bonds for those handling center funds and health and accident insurance for staff members are other options that must be explored. Find out what insurance coverage is needed by child care programs in your state.

11. *Written and unwritten contracts.* A record should be kept of all contracts. Even if you don't have a written agreement, keep notes summarizing the terms of any agreement. Keep purchase orders. This helps insure that no obligations will be lost or overlooked. It also makes the annual inventory easier, because you will have a record of the price paid and date purchased. Having these records also facilitates transition when a director leaves and another assumes the position.

12. *Tax-exempt status.* If your center is nonprofit, you will file for tax-exempt status. This means you will not have to pay state sales taxes. Check your state guidelines for this process.

13. *Indemnification.* Ultimately, it is the board of directors who has fiscal responsibility for the program. The board of directors should enact an Indemnification Resolution. Under this no officer or board member would be held personally responsible for the debt of the corporation.

In some communities child care centers have formed coalitions. They go together to hire an accounting firm and a law firm to handle their financial and legal affairs. For-profit centers often are part of a larger parent company that takes care of these matters for them. However, as the director you need to be aware of the legal and financial requirements for your program and know where to go to get help and advice.

6.8   Discuss what is covered by each type of insurance mentioned in item 10 in the preceding list. Ask someone who is knowledgeable about the insurance needs of child care centers to visit your class or consult with your group. Find out ways your program could be sued and how insurance is needed to protect the center.

6.9   Invite a director to visit your class or go interview a director. Each member of your group should prepare at least two questions to ask regarding legal and financial matters. Compare questions to see that there is no overlap.

Summary

This chapter has focused on the business side of administering a child care center. You have set up a budget, made purchases, and written a grant proposal to request additional funding for your program. You have also discussed where to go to get help for setting up a bookkeeping system. You have also learned about the legal requirements and obligations that must be met in operating a program for children.

References

Child Care Law Center. 1985. Liability insurance guide for child care centers. *Child Care Information Exchange* 43: 32–36.

Click, P. M., and D. W. Click. 1990. *Administration of schools for young children.* 3d ed. Albany, NY: Delmar.

Hildebrand, V. 1990. *Management of child development centers.* 2d ed. New York, NY: Macmillan.

Kotin, L., R. K. Crabtree, and W. F. Aikman. 1981. *Legal handbook for day care centers.* Washington, DC: Department of Health and Human Services.

Minnesota Department of Human Services. 1989. *Licensing requirements for child care centers.* St. Paul, MN: Department of Human Services.

Morris, S. 1990. Catalog buying guide. *Child Care Information Exchange* 71: 51.

Neugebauer, R. 1988. How's business? Status report #4 on for profit child care. *Child Care Information Exchange* 59: 29–34.

Ruopp, R., J. Travers, F. Glantz, and C. Coelen. 1979. *Children at the Center, Volume I.* Cambridge, MA: Abt Associates.

Sackett, R. 1990. Tips on successful buying from early childhood catalogs. *Child Care Information Exchange* 71: 56.

Scallan, P. C. 1987. People giving to people: Executing an annual giving campaign. *Child Care Information Exchange* 54: 9–12.

6.1

Purchase list for one classroom.

Item	Cost	Supplier

Item	Cost	Supplier

Total Cost = _____

6.2

Your group will answer the following questions:

1. What did you learn from purchasing items for one classroom?

2. Where might you look to find some bargains to keep your costs down?

3. What different items would you need for an infant program?

For a toddler program?

For a school-age program?

6.3

Make an annual budget for your program. Follow the outline given or another that will work well for child care programs.

6.4

Income.

1. What will your income be from tuition?

2. What other income will you have?

3. What is your total income?

6.5

What adjustments must be made in your budget?

What budget items did you increase?

What budget items did you decrease?

6.6

The grant proposal.

Your group will write a proposal for your center. First, answer the following questions:

1. How will you use the money? Can you document the need?

2. What objectives do you have that this money might help you reach?

3. How will you evaluate whether you met these objectives or not?

4. Where will future funding be found?

6.7

Revise your budget to reflect the 30 percent increase in funds available.

1. What items will remain the same? Why?

2. What items will be increased? Why?

Financial and Legal Considerations

6.8

Insurance needs.

What information did you get from talking to the insurance consultant?

6.9

Interview with a child care director.

Write down two questions concerning legal and financial matters you wish to ask the director.

1.

2.

Write down what you learned from the director's answers to questions/interview.

7

PHYSICAL SPACE NEEDS FOR THE CENTER

Chapter Outline

Planning the center

The effects of the physical environment on the children and staff

Summary

References

Assignments

7.1 Decide on a location for your program. Discuss regulations that must be met.

7.2 Make a floor plan for your program (individually). With rest of group decide on the best plan for your building.

7.3 Use a rating scale to assess one children's room.

7.4 Arrange one room.

The entrance to the center should be inviting. *Photo by Rob Sklenar*

Planning the Center

Locating the Center

Finding a building to house the child care center or constructing your own building will be one of the first tasks of your group. It is a truism that the three most important considerations in starting a business are "location, location, and location." Some pertinent factors to consider are traffic patterns, accessibility, visibility of the center from the street, future plans for that neighborhood, and the city services such as water, gas, and sewers that are available (Torrence and Harris 1989). Zoning ordinances that govern the location would also be important to know. To serve families with young children, the center must be near where they live and/or work. Real estate agencies and/or state small business services may be able to help you. A needs assessment (as outlined in chapter 2) would help to establish the viability of a child care center in the location you have chosen. You may need to relocate your proposed center based on the research you have done.

State and Local Building Regulations

In most states the space and equipment requirements are clearly delineated in the licensing regulations. Find out what the regulations are that would apply to your center.

States require that all child care facilities comply with local fire, health, building, and zoning ordinances. Centers are expected to provide documentation that they are in compliance when applying for the initial license.

As a general rule centers must be located at ground level, have thirty-five square feet of usable indoor space per child, and have two or more exits. They must have one toilet and sink for each fifteen children, have a separate kitchen, and be adequately heated and cooled. Safety and sanitation rules must be followed.

Outdoor space must provide seventy-five square feet for each of the children who use it at any one time. It must be well maintained.

Infants have special spatial needs. They need separate areas for diapering, food preparation, and sleeping. All regulations must be taken into consideration before any building plans can be finalized.

Leasing Space versus Building

An alternative to building is to lease commercial space or use community facilities such as schools or churches. The advantage of leasing is that it requires a smaller investment of capital. Stephens (1987a, 1987b) has outlined some of the benefits and drawbacks of leasing (see the following chart).

Benefits	**Drawbacks**
Community facilities often have excellent locations.	Landlord-tenant relations can be problematic.
Landlords may allow for expansion without long-term commitment.	Joint usage of space can be a problem.
	Landlords may not want to lease to for-profit centers.
Many old schools or churches are ideally suited to child care.	Landlords may not allow a sign or publicity. This may limit your identity and growth.
Rent can sometimes be based on enrollment or can be renegotiated periodically.	

The Effects of the Physical Environment on the Children and Staff

Elizabeth Prescott and her associates have studied the effects of the physical environment on children and staff in day care centers (Prescott and David 1977; Prescott and Jones 1972; Prescott, Jones, and Kritchevsky 1972). Center size, design, aesthetics, and the use of both indoor and outdoor space all have implications for the quality of the program. Poorly designed centers, where there is very little consideration for the psychological and educational needs of children and the adults that care for them, can become "warehouses" or "institutions" (MacDonald 1990). Greenman (1988) has written a book that should be consulted by anyone planning to build or renovate an existing building to use as a child care center. He has tips for making environments that take into consideration the needs of infants, toddlers, and preschoolers as well as those of the adults that care for them. He has practical ideas for storing materials, arranging rooms, creating outdoor spaces, and locating, designing, and equipping the center.

The environment of a child care center is much more than just the physical attributes of the building or the dimensions and decor of the rooms. It also includes the human environment. How the staff interact with children, how they arrange the room to meet their needs and those of children, and how they structure daily activities are all part of the center environment and cannot be overlooked when talking about the physical space. There is no substitute for well-trained and compensated staff who understand child development and early childhood curriculum and can make design decisions based on what they want to happen in their center. Harms and Clifford (1980) and Harms, Cryer, and Clifford (1990) have developed two helpful rating scales that assess both the physical and care-giving environments of programs for infants and toddlers and for preschoolers. The following chart, based on the *Infant/Toddler Environment Rating Scale*, lists the areas that are evaluated.

- A. Furnishings and Display for Children
    1. Furnishings for routine care
    2. Use of furnishings for learning activities
    3. Furnishings for relaxation and comfort
    4. Room arrangement
    5. Display for children
- B. Personal Care Routines
    6. Greeting/departing
    7. Meals/snacks
    8. Nap
    9. Diapering/toileting
    10. Personal grooming
    11. Health practices
    12. Health policy
    13. Safety practice
    14. Safety policy
- C. Listening and Talking
    15. Informal use of language
    16. Books and pictures
- D. Learning Activities
    17. Eye-hand coordination
    18. Active physical play
    19. Art
    20. Music and movement
    21. Blocks
    22. Pretend play
    23. Sand and water play
    24. Cultural awareness
- E. Interaction
    25. Peer interaction
    26. Adult-child interaction
    27. Discipline
- F. Program Structure
    28. Schedule of daily activities
    29. Supervision of daily activities
    30. Staff cooperation
    31. Provisions for exceptional children
- G. Adult Needs
    32. Adult personal needs
    33. Opportunities for professional growth
    34. Adult meeting area
    35. Provisions for parents

7.1 Discuss the number of children you propose to serve in your center, the site you want to use, and the amount of money you think you will have available to build. If you have an existing building in mind, discuss what renovations would need to be done to make it usable as a child care center. Find out the local building codes and/or state regulations for child care facilities. How will you make certain you are in compliance?

7.2 Each member of your group will make a floor plan for your child care center. Try several preliminary sketches; then choose one to put on a large sheet of tagboard. Clearly label all areas indicating how many children will be in each room. Most state licensing requirements indicate the maximum allowable group size. Check these before beginning. Following are some questions to guide your planning.

1. Have you planned the total site well? Is there enough room for a playground? Is the landscaping designed to complement the building? Is the parking area large enough for cars of the staff, parents, and visitors?

2. Is the entrance area inviting? Is there room to greet parents and children? Is there an area near the entrance that parents can use to wait for their children, read notices, check out parenting materials?

3. Are the children's rooms large without being barnlike? Does each have its own bathroom, sink, and water fountain? Can the room be arranged in several different ways? Do the windows give good light and a view of the outside world for the children? Do they have blinds or fireproof curtains that can be used to darken the room? Is the floor covered in tile or other material that can be easily cleaned? Are there well-anchored area rugs or some part of the room that is carpeted?

4. Is there a kitchen that is separate from the children's areas? Is it large enough for preparing meals? Is there room for a commercial refrigerator and dishwasher? Is there adequate storage space? With supervision, could children use the kitchen for preparing snacks?

5. Is there adequate storage space for program materials, children's and adults' personal belongings, office supplies, cleaning and maintenance materials, and food and cooking paraphernalia?

6. Do infants have a sleeping space or room? Do older children have room for cots? Can the children's rooms be made quiet and restful for sleeping?

7. Is there adequate administrative space? Are there places for private conferences? Do teachers have a place to prepare materials? Is there a staff lounge? Are there bathrooms for adults?

8. Is there a place to isolate a sick child until parents can come?

9. Is there room for furnace, hot water heater, washer and dryer, dishwasher, or other appliances?

10. Do playgrounds have both sun and shade, a good fence, a variety of surfaces, a view of the outside world, a drinking fountain, an accessible bathroom, a place for storing wheel-toys and other playground equipment?

11. Is the design of the center pleasant? Are the interior walls clean and repainted when necessary? Are there corridors that promote an easy flow of traffic without taking up too much space?

In a research project using the *Early Childhood Environment Rating Scale* to rate twenty-one child care centers in southeastern Pennsylvania, Benham, Miller, and Kontos (1988) found that centers rated lowest in facilitation for free play and recognition of individual differences. Lacking were areas where children could play, work, or relax alone. Few materials represented minority, ethnic, or racial groups. Planning for exceptional children was also not in evidence. Centers also scored low on the *adult needs* subscale; separate adult meeting areas and facilities for adult personal needs were generally lacking.

Beyond the necessity for good design in the planning of the entire center, each room must be arranged with the needs of the children and staff in mind. Preschoolers, for example, need places where they can be active and move around freely. They also need quiet spaces where they can get away from the rest of the group. Infants need a separate food/formula preparation area as well as other specific spaces. Traffic patterns must be examined to see how they increase or decrease the movement of children and teachers. If possible, consult Greenman's (1988) chapter on infants/toddlers' needs and preschoolers' needs for learning environments before doing the next assignment.

7.3 Visit a child care program. Using one of the environmental rating scales (Harms and Clifford 1980 or Harms, Cryer, and Clifford 1990) provided by the instructor rate the environment in one room.

7.4 Pick out one room in the center you have designed. Make a list of the space needs of the age group you have chosen and the adults that care for them. Show how you will arrange this room. First show where all the built-in features will be (sinks, toilets, closets, etc.). Then show how you will arrange the furniture. What learning centers (block corner, housekeeping area, art center, etc.) will you have? How will sleeping arrangements be made? Where will children eat?

Summary

Finding a good location for your program near the population you wish to serve is important. The program must be in compliance with local and state building regulations that are specifically designed for child care centers. Making the environment a pleasant place for children and their families and for the staff who work with them is essential in a well-functioning center.

References

Benham, N., T. Miller, and S. Kontos. 1988. Pinpointing staff training needs in child care centers. *Young Children* 43(4): 9–16.

Greenman, J. 1988. *Caring spaces, learning places: Children's environments that work.* Redmond, WA: Exchange Press, Inc.

Harms, T., and R. M. Clifford. 1980. *Early childhood environment rating scale.* New York: Teachers College Press.

Harms, T., D. Cryer, and R. M. Clifford. 1990. *Infant/toddler environment rating scale.* New York: Teachers College Press.

MacDonald, D. 1990. Architecture for kids: Deinstitutionalizing the design of child-care centers. *Day Care and Early Education* 17(4): 4–8.

Prescott, E., and T. G. David. 1977. The effects on children of the physical environment of day care. In *Policy issues in day care: Summaries of 21 papers,* 117–121. Washington, DC: Department of Health, Education, and Welfare.

Prescott, E., and E. Jones. 1972. *Day care as a child rearing environment, volume I.* Washington, DC: NAEYC.

Prescott, E., E. Jones, and S. Kritchevsky. 1972. *Day care as a child rearing environment, volume II.* Washington, DC: NAEYC.

Stephens, K. 1987a. Leasing space for your child care program: Considering community facilities. *Child Care Information Exchange* 57: 37–40.

———. 1987b. Leasing commercial space for your child care program. *Child Care Information Exchange* 58: 15–18.

Torrence, D., and D. J. Harris. 1989. So you want to open a child care center? Advice for the beginner. *Day Care and Early Education* 16: 21–25.

7.1

Discuss the factors that must be taken into consideration in designing or renovating the space for your group's child care center.

1. The site you want to use.

2. How many children you will be serving.

3. Renovations that need to be done to an already existing building.

4. If you are building a new facility, regulations that must be followed.

7.2

Make a preliminary sketch of a floor plan for your center. First determine how many groups you will have based on the group-size requirements in your state.

7.3

After having visited a room in an actual child care center and rating the environment, what conclusions did you make?

1. What did you see as the strengths of the environment?

    a.

    b.

    c.

    d.

2. In what areas did you find weaknesses?

    a.

    b.

    c.

    d.

3. What recommendations would you make for improving the environment?

    a.

    b.

    c.

    d.

7.4

Design one room in your center. Make a sketch of your room here. Put in all the furniture and arrange for learning centers. If the room is for infants and toddlers, show what different areas will be included.

Design one room (continued). Answer the following questions.

1. What are the space needs of this age group?

    a.

    b.

    c.

    d.

2. What are the space needs of the adult caregivers?

    a.

    b.

    c.

    d.

3. How will sleeping areas be arranged?

4. Where will children eat?

5. Where are the quiet spaces for individual children?

8

THE CHILDREN'S PROGRAM

Chapter Outline

Planning the curriculum

Writing a child care plan

Children's records

Summary

References

Assignments

8.1   Discuss developmentally appropriate practices.

8.2   Make a daily schedule for a preschool classroom.

8.3   Design an activity/lesson plan for teachers to use in curriculum planning.

8.4   Write a child care plan including curriculum guidelines, naps and rest, and behavior guidance parameters.

8.5   Review goals, purpose, and philosophy statements to see if the child care plan is consistent with these.

8.6   Prepare a registration form for your center that will include most of the information your state requires.

The director oversees the program for children. She is involved in deciding with teachers what the curriculum will be, how discipline will be handled, and how meals, naps and other routines will be carried out. Most child care programs serve more than just one age group. Infants and toddlers, preschoolers, and school-age children have different developmental characteristics and needs. Each group will require a different approach based on its age and developmental level in deciding what activities and routines will be included in each daily session. Click and Click (1990) have a chapter on planning with preschoolers and another that addresses the needs of infants, toddlers, and older children.

Planning the Curriculum

Everything that happens in the center is part of the curriculum. Children will learn not only from the educational activities that teachers plan, but also from many other influences in the center environment. The way adults interact with children and with each other, the company of other children, the physical setting, the way parents feel about the center, and many other factors combine to determine what each child will learn.

Caldwell (1989) has pointed out that child care and early childhood education are indivisible. All high-quality programs for young children combine the best features of both. The best programs include protective care of children and an educational program designed to encourage and facilitate children's development in all domains—social, cognitive, physical and emotional. A comprehensive, integrated program that meets the needs of children and parents is the goal of every good center.

Working with staff to reach this goal is a primary role for every director. Hiring qualified people to work with children, providing many diverse opportunities for training for the staff, and monitoring each room to see what is being taught and how staff treat children is a big part of the director's job. Together with the staff and the board, she must work out a philosophy that will guide every adult who works in the program and who interacts in any way with the children. Support staff such as cooks, secretaries, and janitors must be included in discussions of the purposes, goals, and philosophy so they will understand how their performances affect the program. It is not enough for the director to have the knowledge and skills needed to make the program work. She must impart this know-how to her staff and motivate them to share in the vision. They are the ones, after all, who work directly with children and their families.

Although in some programs a head teacher oversees the work of the teaching staff, it is generally the director with a background in early childhood education who does this. She provides time for teachers to plan and meets with individual teachers to go over these plans on a weekly basis. She provides expertise and guidance for those in training. She solicits input from parents, other professionals, and authorities from the child care field. She keeps current on the research and trends in the discipline. She shares her knowledge with others through staff meetings or through individual conversations.

Whether it is the director or the head teacher who supervises the teaching staff, that person will need training in child development and early childhood education to help the staff plan a "developmentally appropriate curriculum" (Bredekamp 1987; Kuykendall 1990). There has been a major push in the early childhood field to abandon the "back to basics" and "concentration on academics" philosophies that were emphasized in the 1970s and 1980s and to shape the curriculum much more by what has been discovered in the last twenty-five years about how young children learn. In developmentally appropriate practice children are encouraged to interact with materials, events, and people in their environment through play and active learning. Whole group lessons with the teacher doing most of the talking are kept at a minimum. Encouraging peer interaction, stressing the process rather than the product, and matching the curriculum to the child (not vice versa) are all part of the developmentally appropriate curriculum. Even very young children are seen as competent, responsible, and able to make choices that guide their own learning. Rigid schedules and routines are not allowed to interrupt the flow of play or the finishing of projects. There is no one right way to carry out a task. Curriculum areas are integrated into large time blocks and noise and messiness are seen as natural outgrowths of meaningful activity. Often there is some unifying theme or project for older

Children need time to think about what they will do next. This teacher waits patiently. *Photo by Steve Hermann*

preschoolers and school-age children (Katz and Chard 1989). Child development theory is the framework for making curriculum decisions.

Providing resource books that help teachers set up the environment and plan activities that take into consideration both group and individual needs can aide staff in providing a supportive learning climate for young children. Special training is needed for working with infants and toddlers, because their way of experiencing the world is developmentally different from that of preschoolers. Although school-age and preschool children need some structure and planning in their daily schedule, toddlers need a very flexible schedule. Each infant is on his or her own schedule and the adults must accommodate themselves to the infants' needs. Children with disabilities may need special adaptations in the curriculum. Requiring teachers to make a weekly or monthly written plan for their groups and going over it with them can ensure that planning is taking place and that it is appropriate for the children's developmental level.

8.1   Become familiar with the NAEYC publication, *Developmentally appropriate practice in early childhood programs serving children from birth through age 8*, edited by Bredekamp (1987). In your group discuss what the director or head teacher could do to help staff members use more developmentally appropriate practices in the following situations.

The Children's Program

1. The child care workers in the infant room go about their care-giving routines without talking to the babies.
2. Adults working with toddlers take away children's special blankets or other transition objects or expect children to share them with others.
3. Toddlers are expected to eat, sleep, or participate in other activities as a group.
4. Adults are constantly giving toddlers negative feedback such as "don't do that" or "No."
5. Preschoolers are expected to color predrawn patterns or to make an art object that follows the teacher's model.
6. Teachers communicate with parents only when their child is having a problem.
7. Preschool teachers expect children to sit still and listen or do paper and pencil tasks. Children spend much time passively waiting, listening, and sitting.
8. School-age child care duplicates the activities that children have been doing in their elementary classrooms.

8.2 Make up a daily schedule for a preschool room. Include time for routines such as snacks, meals, and naptime. Decide what blocks of time teachers should plan.

8.3 Set up an outline for an activity plan that preschool teachers could use in planning the curriculum for their group of children. Will a theme or unit approach be used? How will these be chosen? Will children's interests, cultural backgrounds, and developmental levels be taken into consideration?

Although this workbook focuses on administration, the importance of the curriculum and what is happening with the children cannot be overemphasized. A child care center is not just a babysitter for the convenience of parents who must work; it is a place where children spend most of their waking hours. They learn to talk, think, and feel at the center. They develop their physical skills. They learn how to get along with others. Their intellectual appetites are stimulated. The care and education they get here helps determine who these children will be as adults.

Writing A Child Care Plan

It is the director's job to keep parents and anyone else who is interested informed about the curriculum. Parents are usually eager to know what their child will be doing and learning. Many states require that a plan for the care of young children be worked out in writing and be made available to parents, licensing personnel, staff members, and the general public. Check your state regulations to see what is required. The following questions are based on the Child Care Program Plan, Naps and Rest, and Behavior Guidance sections of Licensing Requirements for Child Care Centers put out by the Minnesota Department of Human Services (1989).

1. Is there a mandate that children should be supervised at all times?
2. Have you described the age categories and number of children to be served in the program?
3. Are the hours and days of operation clearly stated?
4. Have you described the philosophy, goals, and purposes of your program and the methods you will use to reach these?

5. Have you specified activities that will be used to promote the intellectual, social, emotional, and physical development of each child in a manner consistent with the child's cultural background?

6. Have you specified how each child's development will be documented in the child's record and conveyed to the parents during conferences?

7. Have you provided a daily schedule of both indoor and outdoor activities, both quiet and active, and teacher-directed and child-initiated activities? Prepare a typical schedule for a preschool child.

8. What interest centers will you have? Describe which ones will be set up in a preschool room and give a rationale for each. How often will they be changed, and why?

9. Will parents be consulted at enrollment time about naps/rest for the child? What will you say if a parent of a 3-year-old doesn't want the child to nap so he will sleep better at home?

10. Will some provision be made for children who have rested quietly, but do not sleep?

11. How will cots and cribs be arranged for naptime?

12. What regulations will govern the use of cribs?

13. How will bedding be provided and cleaned?

14. How will behavior be guided?

15. How will you ensure that children are provided with a positive model of acceptable behavior?

16. How will behavior guidance be tailored to the developmental level of the children of the center?

17. How will children be redirected or given acceptable alternatives to problem behavior?

18. How will the safety of children and adults be protected?

19. What will be the immediate and directly related consequences for a child's unacceptable behavior?

20. When a child's behavior is persistently unacceptable what will be done? Will the behavior be observed and recorded with staff responses? Will a plan for dealing with this behavior be developed with parents, staff, and other professionals (when appropriate)? In case the child cannot be accommodated in your program, what will your discharge policy be?

21. What actions of staff members will be prohibited? These might include all forms of physical punishment; emotional abuse; separation from group except under certain circumstances; punishment for lapses in toilet habits; withholding of light, warmth, clothing, or medical care as punishment; use of physical restraints (other than when confinement is necessary to protect a child or others from injury); or use of mechanical restraints.

22. What procedure will be made for separation from the group? When will this be used? When will the child be returned to the group? How will these time-outs be recorded? Will parents be consulted if a child has more than three in one day? How will you ensure that infants under a certain age will not be separated from the group as a means of behavior guidance?

23. How will special behavior guidance procedures be worked out for children with disabilities and/or mental retardation?

24. Will parents be consulted about their child's eating habits?

Note that these guidelines do not cover drop-in programs, sick care or night care, or infant/toddler or school-age care. These types of programs would have other regulations that must be met. Child care for children with special needs would also require separate considerations.

8.4 Write a child care plan for your program after referring to your state's guidelines. If your state's regulations are very general, use the previous questions to help you formulate your policies.

8.5 Once you have a rough draft of your center's child care plan, go back over your goals, purpose, and philosophy statements to see if what you have written is consistent with it.

Children's Records

A confidential file must be maintained on each child in the program. Files are to be made available only to the child, the child's parent or guardian, the child's legal representative, employees of the center, and the state commissioner (of social/human services)—unless the child's parent or guardian has given written consent.

The following items are typically included in each child's file:

1. Name
2. Birth date
3. Address
4. Information about the child's parents, including where they can be reached when the child is at the center
5. Emergency numbers if parents cannot be reached
6. The child's hours of attendance
7. Names of those authorized to take child from the center
8. Health and dental care sources
9. Health form and immunization information signed by child's health care provider
10. Permission forms for administering emergency treatment or first aid
11. Permission to give syrup of ipecac (to induce vomiting in cases of suspected poisoning and given only under the directions of a physician or poison control center)
12. Allergy information
13. Permission to use diaper/sunscreen products
14. Permission for each field trip
15. Permission to involve children in public relations or research
16. Documentation of any dietary, religious, or medical restraints on child's activities
17. Date and summary of information provided to the parent at conferences

8.6 Check your state's licensing requirements to see if any additional information must be kept in each child's file. Design a registration form that would include the information and permissions you are required to have. Discuss what measures you will take to protect the confidentiality of these files.

Summary

The director supervises the children's program. She helps teachers plan and carry out the curriculum. She writes a child care plan to give to parents and others and works with staff to see that it is followed. She tries to keep the plan consistent with the goals, purposes, and philosophy of the program. She manages children's records.

References

Bredekamp, S., ed. 1987. *Developmentally appropriate practice in early childhood programs serving children from birth through age 8 (expanded edition).* Washington, DC: NAEYC.

Caldwell, B. M. 1989. A comprehensive model for integrating child care and early childhood education. *Teachers College Record* 90:3.

Click, P. M., and D. W. Click. 1990. *Administration of schools for young children.* 3d ed. Albany, NY: Delmar.

Katz, L. G., and S. C. Chard. 1989. *Engaging children's minds: The project approach.* Norwood, NJ: Ablex.

Kuykendall, J. 1990. Child development: Directors shouldn't leave home without it! *Young Children* 45(5): 47–50.

Minnesota Department of Human Services. 1989. *Licensing requirements for child care centers.* St. Paul, MN: Department of Human Services.

8.1

Discuss what the director/head teacher could do to promote developmentally appropriate practices in the following situations. What were some of the suggestions from your groups?

1. Getting caregivers to talk to babies.

2. Toddler caregivers taking their blankets or other transition objects.

3. Toddlers expected to act as a group.

4. Adults giving mostly negative feedback to toddlers.

5. Preschoolers expected to follow patterns/models.

6. Teachers communicating only negative comments to parents.

7. Preschoolers expected to sit, wait, and listen.

8. The curriculum in school-age care is similar to that in elementary classroom.

8.2

Plan a schedule for preschoolers. Include routines such as arrival, meals and snacks, and naptimes. What times will be used for learning activities, indoor and outdoor play?

8.3

Design an activity/lesson plan that preschool teachers could use in planning the curriculum for their group. Be sure that this plan is geared to this age group and not to older, elementary-age children. Will a theme/unit approach be used? How will these be chosen? Will children's interests, cultural backgrounds, and developmental levels be taken into consideration?

8.4

Write a child care plan following your state's guidelines or those given in this workbook.

Child care plan (continued).

8.5

After writing your center's child care plan and going over your goals, purpose, and philosophy statements, what changes have you made and why?

8.6

What additional information does your state require be kept for each child? Write a draft of a registration form for your center that would include the information you need from parents.

9

HEALTH AND SAFETY IN THE CENTER

Chapter Outline

Keeping the children and staff safe and healthy

Health care consultants

Summary

References

Assignments

9.1   Develop emergency and accident policies.

9.2   Develop health policies.

9.3   Discuss where to get health consultants.

9.4   Plan a unit on health or safety.

Keeping the Children and Staff Safe and Healthy

When parents entrust their children to a program, they expect that the staff will do everything they can to ensure that the children will be protected from danger. Whenever possible, illnesses and accidents will be avoided. When emergencies do occur, the staff will be prepared to deal with them.

Dr. Susan Aronson, a pediatrician who writes a bimonthly health column in the *Child Care Information Exchange* and has written a comprehensive book about the health and safety needs of children in center care, wrote that ". . . children need more than simple protection from hazards. They need activities that promote healthy development and prevent problems with growth, body system functioning, learning and social and emotional competence. Health promotion includes traditional health care services such as check ups, immunization, screening tests, diagnostic services, treatment. In addition, health promotion should include good nutrition, dental health measures such as fluoridation and dental hygiene, opportunities to develop fitness habits, and opportunities to develop mental health skills" (Aronson 1991, 2). She suggested that programs, because of limitations of resources, must focus their efforts on "minimizing injuries, preventing and managing infectious diseases, and modifying features of the environment and program to promote health" (Aronson 1991, 3). Although it is impossible to control all the factors that are potentially dangerous to young children without undue restrictions on their activities, staff members can take reasonable precautions to prevent accidents and to avoid the spread of disease.

Staff need some guidelines and training for recognizing when a child becomes ill at the center or when an emergency situation exists. Being aware that children who are sick often exhibit certain symptoms such as lack of appetite, change in skin color, lethargy, elevation of fever, rash, complaints of stomach pains, and so on can help them identify the sick child. Isolating the child from the other children, contacting the parents or other designated person to pick up the child, and notifying other parents if their children have been exposed to a contagious disease is required of center staff. Few centers have the medically trained staff and facilities to care for children who are ill. Insisting that all the teaching staff have current certification in First Aid and child CPR will help ensure that they will be alert to accidents and know the correct procedures to follow should an emergency occur.

The Need for A Written Plan

The center should have a written plan for handling the routine health and safety of the children. There should also be written procedures to follow for any emergency situations that arise. "By developing and enforcing sound health and accident policies, programs are protecting the well-being of children in their care" (Stephens 1991, 2). Stephens suggested consulting state licensing requirements as well as resources such as Aronson's book and the NAEYC publication, *Healthy Young Children: A Manual for Programs* by Kendrick, Kaufmann, and Messenger (1991). Stephens also had several strategies for helping parents realize the importance of following these policies. Centers can display health posters, books, and videos; hold workshops on health and safety issues; and include items in the parents' newsletter about health concerns.

Emergency and Accident Policies

9.1 Develop emergency and accident policies using your state's guidelines. If your state requirements are very general, you may wish to consult the following list of questions to help you formulate your center's policies.

1. What are the procedures for administering first aid? Will all staff members be required to be certified in First Aid and CPR?

2. What safety rules will be set up for children and staff to follow in avoiding injuries, burns, poisoning, choking, suffocation, and traffic and pedestrian accidents?

3. How often will inspections by the fire marshall, housing/engineering inspector, and health department be made?

4. What are the procedures for fire prevention? What will the staff do in case of a fire? Included here might be how often fire drills are held and how they are logged, identifying the primary and secondary exits, instructions on the use of a fire extinguisher, and what training staff will be given to carry out these procedures.

5. What procedures will be carried out in the event of a blizzard, tornado, earthquake, or other natural disaster? Are drills necessary to teach children and staff where to go and what to do?

6. What procedures will be followed when a child is missing?

7. How will children be protected when an unauthorized or incapacitated person or one suspected of child abuse attempts to pick up a child or if no one comes to pick up a child? What will happen when parents are habitually late or several hours late in picking up their child/children. Will this be reported as child neglect?

8. Where will children be taken who require emergency medical care? How will parents be notified?

9. What records will be kept for persons injured or involved in an incident at the center? These should include the name and age of the persons involved, date and place of the accident, injury or incident, type of injury, action taken by staff, and to whom it was reported.

10. Will the center be required to have battery-operated flashlights and portable radio to use in emergency situations?

11. What provisions will be made for periodic screening for hazardous conditions in the center both indoors and outdoors? What kind of daily inspection will be made?

12. What emergency numbers will be posted by the telephone? The Texas Department of Human Services (1985) requires that a telephone be accessible to all staff and not be a pay phone. The department mandates the inclusion of numbers for an ambulance or emergency medical services, police or sheriff's departments, fire department, poison control center, local child protection services office or child abuse hotline, and the center (with address). In addition centers must keep numbers where parents can be reached and the numbers of each child's physician as designated by parents accessible to the telephone and to all staff. The number for the state licensing consultant should also be posted.

13. What provisions will be made that ensure that young children are under adult supervision at all times when they are at the center? How will field trips be handled?

Playgrounds are the scene of many injuries to young children. It is essential to see that playgrounds are well designed with equipment that meets the developmental needs of young children and that they be well maintained. Since the major cause of serious injuries are falls onto hard surfaces, playgrounds must use soft materials such as sand or wood chips as a base under certain pieces of equipment. Frost and Wortham (1988) include a safety checklist, which gives further ideas for preventing playground accidents.

This caregiver's lap is a haven of security for this child. She will protect him. *Photo by Steve Hermann*

Health Policies

9.2 Develop **health policies** using state requirements. Check this list to see that the following issues are covered.

1. What evidence will the center require at the time of admission that a child is physically able to take part in the program? This might be a signed statement from the child's health care source. Usually a time since the last physical assessment is specified. Under what conditions will exemptions be made? After what period of time will children need to be reexamined and will this vary with age of child?

2. What documentation will be needed to show that immunizations are current? What medical or religious reasons might warrant exemption?

3. What sanitation procedures will be followed in general building maintenance, food preparation, diapering and toileting children, disinfecting toys? How will staff be trained to use sanitary practices?

4. How will staff handle a child who becomes sick at the center? Will sick children be excluded? How will parents be notified?

5. How will children be protected from others who are ill? Will an isolation room be available? Will sick staff members be excluded? Will smoking be banned?

6. How will other parents be notified of contagious diseases? Will state and local health authorities be notified of the occurrence of certain diseases?

7. Will the center administer medicine to children? If so, how will it be done? Will written permission of parents be needed to administer other products besides prescription medicines? Will the administration of all medicines be recorded? How will these medicines and/or products be stored?

8. Will a first aid kit and book be available? What items will the kit contain? Who will be trained to administer first aid?

9. Will pets be permitted at the center? If so, how will they be inoculated and cared for to protect children's health?

Programs that are licensed to care for children who are sick have special requirements that must be met. These are not covered in this workbook. If you are interested in providing such a service, consult your state licensing agent.

Children who come to the center may have physical disabilities, developmental delays, hearing/vision deficits, or chronic medical conditions that have gone undetected. Often the director or teaching staff are the first professionals to see that child besides the pediatrician. Many parents do not have enough information about children's normal development to be able to see that something may be wrong with their child. They may suspect a problem but be unwilling to admit that their child may need special help. The center staff must be aware of resources in the community who can provide screening, diagnostic testing, and treatment and help parents to get the help needed.

In addition to caring for the children's physical health, the center must provide an environment that is conducive to good mental health for both the children and adults. Everyone deserves to be accepted and valued. Children need to be cared for by adults who genuinely enjoy spending the long day with them and who interact and speak with children in ways that foster their positive self-esteem (Kostelnik, Stein, and Whiren 1988). Children need help in learning to separate from their parents, in learning to control their own behavior, in finding acceptable ways to express their emotions, and in getting along with their peers. They may need special consideration when dealing with crisis situations in their families such as divorce (Skeen and McKenry 1980) or death (Honig 1986). Children who have been abused can be helped to view the center as a safe place (Caughey 1991). The child care center can provide a therapeutic setting for children who come from homes that are disorganized and overstimulating or are neglectful and understimulating.

Being a child care worker is an intense job that necessarily requires emotional involvement of the adults who care for young children. Staff members need reassurance that their job is important to the children and families they serve and to the larger society. Much of what child care workers do to bolster children's self-esteem and integrate them into the group can be viewed as preventive mental health. Staff need to be told often that what they do is valued. Besides adequate remuneration, teachers need time away from the children for breaks and a generous policy for vacations and personal days off.

Staff Health

The director and staff can take measures to ensure their own health and promote general sanitation at the center (Seefeldt and Barbour 1990). Teaching staff who have infectious illnesses should not be working with young children. The director can insist that staff have adequate time off to recover and may ask for a doctor's permission slip before a staff member who had an infectious illness may come back to work. Providing sick leave with pay can ensure that staff will follow this policy.

Health Care Consultants

Many states require that each center have a health consultant who reviews these policies yearly (monthly if infants are served) and certifies that they are adequate to protect the health and safety of the children in care. You will need to contract with a physician, registered nurse, or other approved health care consultant to do this on an annual basis and provide the state with written documentation. Programs that take infants will need separate health policies for them. Infant rooms must undergo monthly inspection.

If the child care center you operate is very large (more than one hundred fifty children), you may want to hire a full-time licensed practical nurse or registered nurse to monitor the health of all the children in your program. If your center cannot afford a full-time health professional, you might consider contracting with a part-time person or with a health agency to spend a certain amount of time each month. They could make certain immunizations are given at the appropriate times, oversee sanitary measures employed by the staff, work with parents about their family's health concerns, and keep health records current.

The center may also wish to contract with a licensed psychologist. This person would be concerned with the mental health and behavior of both the staff and the children and their families. A psychologist can help parents and staff prevent practices that might be detrimental to a child's emotional development. They could help the staff deal with their feelings about the intensive and demanding work they do with children. They could do some parent education about normal development and parenting skills. They could consult with the staff about particular children and help plan specific programs for individual children. They could work directly with children doing diagnostic testing or therapy.

9.3 Write down where you might go in your community to find the services of a health care professional or psychologist. Would any of these services be available to your program through the local social services agency or school district? Also describe when and why you might engage health consultants.

If your program is not large enough to warrant hiring consultants for these services, it becomes the director's job to supervise these tasks either by delegating them to qualified staff members or doing them herself.

Health and Safety in the Curriculum

Keeping children healthy and safe is a primary goal of a child care center and is basic to any program. The welfare of the children is of paramount concern. The curriculum should reflect this. Even very young children can be taught the simple rules of hygiene and safety (Hendrick 1990). The teaching staff can set learning goals for children related to health based on the children's developmental levels (Broman 1982; Jurs and Mangili 1989). For example, preschoolers can be expected to wash hands before eating and after toileting and can demonstrate the correct procedure for brushing teeth. They can also learn safety procedures if they are involved in an active way. One suggestion for teaching first aid is to have children practice on a teddy bear or doll (Comer 1987).

9.4 Choose one of the following ways to include health and safety in the curriculum:

1. Plan a unit on dental health that could be used with a group of five- and six-year-olds.

2. Plan a unit for preschoolers that deals with how their heart pumps blood that carries food and oxygen to the rest of their body.

3. Design an active way to teach elementary-age children about traffic safety.

Teachers can make a daily health check part of the morning routine. Often parents are in a hurry to get to work or school and do not realize that their young child is not feeling well. Checking to see if the child has a fever, looking at the chest area for a rash, checking the neck for swollen glands, questioning parents about vomiting or appetite loss could be done in any suspected child illness case.

Summary

The child care center has an obligation to protect young children from illnesses and accidents. A written plan is the best way to guarantee that proper procedures will be followed. The program needs to engage health care consultants to monitor the program. Health and safety are important elements that should be included in the curriculum for children of all ages.

References

Aronson, S. S. 1991. *Health and safety in child care.* New York: HarperCollins.

Broman, B. L. 1982. *The early years in childhood education.* 2d ed. Prospect Heights, IL: Waveland Press.

Caughey, C. 1991. Becoming the child's ally—Observations in a classroom for children who have been abused. *Young Children* 46(4): 22–28.

Comer, D. E. 1987. *Developing safety skills with young children: A commonsense, nonthreatening approach.* Albany, NY: Delmar.

Frost, J. L., and S. C. Wortham. 1988. The evolution of American playgrounds. *Young Children* 43(5): 19–28.

Hendrick, J. 1990. *Total learning: Developmental curriculum for the young child.* Columbus, OH: Merrill.

Honig, A. S. 1986. Stress and coping in children. *Young Children* 41(4): 50–63.

Jurs, J., and L. Mangili. 1989. Having fun with health: Providing activities for young children. *Day Care and Early Education* 16(4): 18–20.

Kendrick, A. S., R. Kaufmann, and K. P. Messenger. 1991. *Healthy young children: A manual for programs.* Washington, DC: NAEYC.

Kostelnik, M. J., L. C. Stein, and A. P. Whiren. 1988. Children's self-esteem: The verbal environment. *Childhood Education* 65(1): 29–32.

Seefeldt, C., and N. Barbour. 1990. *Early childhood education: An introduction.* Columbus, OH: Merrill.

Skeen, P., and P. C. McKenry. 1980. The teacher's role in facilitating a child's adjustment to divorce. *Young Children* 35(5): 3–12.

Stephens, K. 1991. Health policies and parents. *First Teacher* 12(5): 2, 13.

Texas Department of Human Services. 1989. *Regulation of child-care facilities.* Austin, TX: Department of Human Services.

9.1

Develop emergency and accident policies for your center using your state's guidelines and those given in this workbook.

9.2

Develop health policies using state requirements. Add others your group deems important.

9.3

What community resources are available to your program for psychological or medical services?

When or why would you contract for their services?

9.4

Choose one of the following ways to include health and safety in the curriculum:

1. Plan a unit for five- and six-year-olds on dental health.

2. Plan a unit for preschoolers on how the heart works and what it does.

3. Find an active way to teach school-age children about traffic safety.

10

NUTRITION AND MEALS

Chapter Outline

Planning the food program

Special food problems

Summary

References

Assignments

10.1 Write a letter of application to the Child and Adult Care Food Program.

10.2 Plan menus for a four-week period.

10.3 Write mealtime guidelines for staff.

10.4 Write a plan for feeding infants and toddlers.

10.5 Write a policy for celebration treats.

10.6 Discuss how staff will be alerted to food allergies.

Planning the Food Program

Another area of the children's program for which the director is responsible is meal and snack planning. Since young children get much of their daily food intake while they are with you, this is an area of great concern for children's health and well-being.

Child and Adult Care Food Program

Public and private nonprofit organizations in child care may participate in the Child and Adult Care Food Program sponsored by the United States Department of Agriculture (USDA). This is often administered through the Department of Education as part of the School Lunch Program. Private, for-profit centers may also qualify if at least 25 percent of the children in the center are receiving compensation under Title XX of the Social Security Act (Kendrick, Kaufmann, and Messenger 1988). If your program is eligible for the Child and Adult Care Food Program, you may also get surplus foods distributed by the USDA or be reimbursed for certain costs. Representatives from this program will come biennially to inspect your center. They look at your menus, sanitation, and the food preparation area. They also go over your record keeping (family incomes, meal counts, food purchasing records). You will need to find out how these food programs are handled in your area.

10.1   Find out who to contact for the Child and Adult Care Food Program in your locale, their address, and the qualifications needed to be eligible; write them a letter requesting that your center be included in their assistance program.

Menu Planning

Because nutrition guidelines put out by the USDA must be followed, food purchased and stored properly, and meals and snacks prepared, menus must be done in advance. Many programs plan on a four-week cycle and have several month-long menus that can be rotated throughout the year. Endres and Rockwell (1990) have extensive information on planning nutritious menus for young children.

Food Resource Management

Buy food and beverages for your program from reputable sources that meet all applicable health codes. Try to find providers who will deliver groceries, milk, and meat to your center. This saves much staff time and is often worth the added expense. Provide proper storage for perishable food items. Be sure freezer and refrigeration units are operating at the right temperatures. Make sure your food preparation area and methods meet health department regulations. Kendrick, Kaufmann, and Messenger's manual (1988) can be consulted for further information.

Many child care programs contract with restaurants or food services outside the center for meals and snacks. You would need to investigate to see if that is a cost-effective and convenient system to use for your center.

10.2 Each member of your group will prepare a menu plan for a four-week period. Included in this plan will be breakfast, morning snack, lunch, and afternoon snack. Include food that would be familiar to different ethnic groups that may be attending your center. Use the following chart as a guide.

Breakfast	A.M. Snack	Lunch	P.M. Snack
1/2 cup fluid milk	Choose two of these four:	Milk	Choose two of these four:
Either a fruit, vegetable, or full-strength juice	Milk	Meat and/or alternative	Milk
Cereal and/or bread equivalent & additional food (optional)	Fruit, vegetable, or full-strength juice	Vegetable or fruit	Meat and/or alternative
	Bread, cereal, or equivalent	Vegetable or fruit	Fruit, vegetable, or full-strength juice
	Meat and/or alternative	Bread or equivalent & additional food (optional)	Bread, cereal, or equivalent

Note: Do not serve milk and fruit juice at the same meal.

Mealtimes

You will want to ensure that mealtime is a pleasant experience for all the adults and children in the center. It should be a time when children can socialize and talk with their friends and caregivers in a relaxing atmosphere. Food should never be withheld from children or used as a reward. Although teachers should encourage children to try all that is offered, they should not force them to eat against their will. Trading foods or taking food from another's plate should be discouraged. Children who say "Yuk" or exhibit distasteful grimaces at certain foods should not be allowed to influence other children's food choices.

Besides providing the necessary nutrients for building healthy bodies, mealtime provides children an opportunity for acquiring nutrition information and for learning how to make wise food choices. Children can become aware of what foods are good for their bodies and what foods to avoid or eat in small quantities. Many of the food habits that are learned at an early age stay with us throughout our lives.

Cooking with young children is fun. Learning how to prepare and serve food is an important part of the preschool and school-age curriculum. Following a recipe, measuring ingredients, figuring out how long to cook different foods, and serving them can be enjoyable and useful skills to know. Finding a cook who is tolerant of having teachers and children invade his or her kitchen occasionally is essential. Most books on early childhood curriculum contain a section on nutrition education and cooking with young children.

The director has a role in creating a good mealtime climate. Staff need to know about practices that are to be followed to make mealtimes enjoyable and relaxing for children and adults. Small groups seated around small tables with an adult sitting with them promotes conversations. Having preschool and school-age children serve themselves family style promotes independence and cuts down on waste. Serving children in their rooms instead of in a large dining hall reduces the noise and chaos. Including foods on the menu that reflect the children's ethnic or cultural backgrounds helps children feel "at home" in the center.

This child is the snack helper for the day. He sets out cups and napkins and helps in cleaning up afterwards.
Photo by Steve Hermann

10.3 In your group discuss how you want the staff at your center to handle mealtime. Consult at least one early childhood curriculum text to get ideas. Write up guidelines that the staff is to follow. For example, should children be encouraged to try all foods?

10.4 If your center serves infants, write a special section for feeding infants and toddlers. *Infant caregiving: A design for training,* by Honig and Lally (1981), is a good reference for setting up a feeding program in infant group care. Read the licensing requirements for your state to see what they want included. What provisions will you make to accommodate mothers who are breastfeeding? Will formula and prepared baby foods be supplied by the parents or the center?

Special Food Problems

Celebrations

Often parents want to supply food that they have prepared at home or purchased for a child's birthday or a holiday party. This can become a problem. When eaten several days out of the month, ice cream cones, cake with frosting, cookies, carbonated soft drinks, pretzels, potato chips, candy, and chewing gum give children empty calories and added sodium and lessen their appetites for nourishing food. Parents who are conscious of children's nutritional needs may object. Food may also be contaminated by being prepared under unsanitary conditions or during shipment.

10.5 How shall birthday and holiday "treats" be handled at your center? Write up a policy statement to be given to parents.

Other Nutritional Concerns

Food Preferences. Children develop strong likes and dislikes to certain foods. Ask the parents about their child's eating habits. Many children who have aversions to some foods often learn to eat them when they see their teachers and other children enjoying them. Children should be encouraged to try new foods, but it should be accepted that each child has some foods he or she does not like.

Food Allergies. Many young children have food allergies. Find out from parents how these allergies usually manifest themselves in the child. Many allergic children experience congestion or irritation in the nose, eyes, throat, chest, or skin. Some experience increased excitability and hyperactivity. Common foods that cause allergic reactions or intolerances are milk sugars (lactose), eggs, wheat flour, citrus fruits, shellfish, nuts, and food additives such as artificial food colorings and salicylates (Kendrick, Kaufmann, and Messenger 1988).

Obesity. The pattern for obesity is set very early and is difficult to reverse. Prevention calls for a multifaceted approach that requires changes in parenting behaviors, calorie intake, and physical activity.

Underweight. Some children, particularly those with handicapping conditions, have difficulty gaining weight normally. Sometimes dietary supplements are given.

Behavior Problems. Children sometimes develop inappropriate eating behaviors. Parents should be involved in designing a plan to change these.

Inborn Metabolism Disorders. Phenylketonuria (PKU) or other disorders such as diabetes require carefully controlled diets. Parents may need to supply special foods.

Anemia. Iron deficiency is common for young children, particularly for those with poor eating habits or children from low-income families. Providing iron-rich foods and several sources of vitamin C (which helps the body utilize iron) in the daily diet can help overcome this.

Further information on special nutritional problems is contained in a manual by Kendrick, Kaufmann, and Messenger (1988).

10.6 In your group discuss how you will alert staff members so that they are aware of a child's food allergies. Will alternative food be supplied for a child who is allergic to or refuses to eat certain foods? by whom?

Summary

This chapter discussed setting up a comprehensive nutritional program for your center that includes menu planning, food preparation, finding and managing food resources, cooking with children, and including nutrition in the children's curriculum. Meals and snacks are planned that will meet nutritional standards. Practices are suggested that will help children enjoy food and give them lifelong eating habits that will be beneficial to their health.

References

Endres, J. B., and R. E. Rockwell. 1990. *Food, nutrition, and the young child.* 3d ed. Columbus, OH: Merrill.

Honig, W. S., and J. R. Lally. 1981. *Infant caregiving: A design for training.* Syracuse, NY: Syracuse University Press.

Kendrick, A. S., R. Kaufmann, and K. P. Messenger. 1988. *Healthy young children: A manual for programs.* Washington, DC: NAEYC.

10.1

Write a letter to the Child and Adult Care Food Program in your locale requesting that your program be included in their assistance program.

10.2

Prepare a four-week menu plan. Include breakfast, morning snack, lunch, and afternoon snack.

(Four weekly menu charts follow.)

Program Name _____

Address _____

Phone _____

Week of: _____

	Monday	Tuesday	Wednesday	Thursday	Friday
BREAKFAST fluid milk fruit, vegetable or full strength juice cereal and /or bread equivalent plus additional food (optional)					
AM SNACK (Choose two of these four) fluid milk fruit, vegetable or full strength juice bread, cereal or equivalent meat and/or alternate					
LUNCH fluid milk meat and/or alternate vegetable or fruit vegetable or fruit bread or equivalent plus additional food (optional)					
PM SNACK (Choose two of these four) fluid milk fruit, vegetable or full strength juice bread, cereal or equivalent meat and/or alternate					

Program Name _____

Address _____

Phone _____

Week of: _____

	Monday	Tuesday	Wednesday	Thursday	Friday
BREAKFAST fluid milk fruit, vegetable or full strength juice cereal and/or bread equivalent plus additional food (optional)					
AM SNACK (Choose two of these four) fluid milk fruit, vegetable or full strength juice bread, cereal or equivalent meat and/or alternate					
LUNCH fluid milk meat and/or alternate vegetable or fruit vegetable or fruit bread or equivalent plus additional food (optional)					
PM SNACK (Choose two of these four) fluid milk fruit, vegetable or full strength juice bread, cereal or equivalent meat and/or alternate					

Program Name _____

Address _____

Phone _____

Week of: _____

	Monday	Tuesday	Wednesday	Thursday	Friday
BREAKFAST fluid milk fruit, vegetable or full strength juice cereal and /or bread equivalent plus additional food (optional)					
AM SNACK (Choose two of these four) fluid milk fruit, vegetable or full strength juice bread, cereal or equivalent meat and/or alternate					
LUNCH fluid milk meat and/or alternate vegetable or fruit vegetable or fruit bread or equivalent plus additional food (optional)					
PM SNACK (Choose two of these four) fluid milk fruit, vegetable or full strength juice bread, cereal or equivalent meat and/or alternate					

Program Name _____
Address _____
Phone _____

Week of: _____

	Monday	Tuesday	Wednesday	Thursday	Friday
BREAKFAST fluid milk fruit, vegetable or full strength juice cereal and/or bread equivalent plus additional food (optional)					
AM SNACK (Choose two of these four) fluid milk fruit, vegetable or full strength juice bread, cereal or equivalent meat and/or alternate					
LUNCH fluid milk meat and/or alternate vegetable or fruit vegetable or fruit bread or equivalent plus additional food (optional)					
PM SNACK (Choose two of these four) fluid milk fruit, vegetable or full strength juice bread, cereal or equivalent meat and/or alternate					

Nutrition and Meals

10.3

Write guidelines for staff to follow at mealtime.

1.

2.

3.

4.

5.

6.

7.

8.

10.4

If your center serves infants and toddlers, write guidelines for caregivers to follow in feeding them.

1.

2.

3.

4.

5.

6.

7.

8.

Will formula and prepared baby foods be supplied by the parents or the center?

What provisions will you make to accommodate mothers who are breastfeeding?

10.5

Write a policy statement to be given to parents concerning how birthday and holiday treats are to be handled.

10.6

List ways your group suggests for alerting staff to child's food allergies.

1.

2.

3.

4.

Will alternative food be supplied for a child who is allergic to or refuses to eat certain foods? by whom?

11

WORKING WITH PARENTS

Chapter Outline

The relationship between the center and the family

Communicating with parents

Other ways to involve parents

Summary

References

Assignments

11.1 Make a year-long plan for including multicultural education in your program.

11.2 Discuss the director's role in multicultural situations.

11.3 Prepare a parent handbook that will include all the policies you will give them when they enroll their child.

11.4 Examine and rate several parent handbooks.

11.5 Write a letter setting up a parent-teacher conference.

11.6 Make a form for teachers to use when conferring with parents about their child.

11.7 Compose a sheet of daily information to be given to parents of infants and toddlers.

11.8 Plan an orientation meeting for parents.

11.9 Schedule other parent events for the year.

11.10 Discuss two other ways to include parents.

A mother brings her three children into the center. She needs to feel welcome there so she can help her children adjust to being away from her. *Photo by Steve Hermann*

The Relationship Between the Center and the Family

The Director and the Parents

Most early childhood teachers learn methods for relating to young children as part of their undergraduate training. They also need skills for relating and communicating with adults, including both staff members and parents.

Parents have a special claim on the director's attention. They entrust their children to the child care center. For parents the director is the embodiment of the program. They hold her responsible for anything that happens to their child and they look to her as a model of how they should act with their child. They expect the director to create a center climate where both they and their child can feel welcome, comfortable, and appreciated. The administrator of any program that involves young children will spend a sizable portion of time working with parents.

Parents can also be a valuable resource for the center. They can serve as advisors on all aspects of the center's functioning and must be consulted on curriculum matters that affect their children (Sale 1984). Parents can also contribute directly to the program by volunteering their time and/or talents. A father who comes to his child's classroom to play the guitar and sing with the children, a mother who accompanies the group on a walk to the train station, a parent who serves on a search committee to hire a new teacher, or a parent who volunteers to repair broken toys or make new paint aprons can all be valuable assets to the program. Coleman (1991) pointed out that "Care should be taken to offer parents a range of support, partnership, and leadership roles" (17). When children see their parents taking part in their center, they feel special. They also get to see their parent in another role, which helps the child's self-esteem.

Parental Involvement

Parental involvement has been shown to be essential to the successful functioning of early childhood programs. Longitudinal studies done on experimental early intervention programs begun in the 1960s demonstrated the important role of parents in working with poor, disadvantaged children (Lazar, Darlington, Murray, Royce, and Snipper 1982). The five characteristics they found for successful intervention included five items that related to parent involvement.

1. Begin intervention as early as possible.
2. Provide services to the parents as well as to the child.
3. Provide frequent home visits.
4. Involve parents in the instruction of the child.
5. Have as few children per teacher as possible.

The linkage between home, school, and community continues to be of primary importance to those concerned with the development of young children. Umansky (1983) stated, "Closer contact between parents and teachers will give each a more complete picture of the child's abilities and improve consistency in working toward desired goals. Most important, perhaps, the child will identify both the school and the home as places to learn, and parents and teachers as sources of learning" (264). Berger (1987) gives a more complete picture of the research on the need for parent involvement and the benefits to both parent and child.

Responding to Parents' Concerns and Feelings

The parent-child relationship is emotionally intense. Parents are generally experiencing many different and conflicting feelings when they bring their child to the child care center for the first time (Leavitt and Eheart 1985). They feel guilt about leaving their child in someone else's care; yet, they want and need employment. They feel anxious about placing their child in a group-care situation. They worry that their child will not get the attention the parents have given him or her. They are not sure they should be entrusting their child to strangers. In many ways parents are experiencing feelings of helplessness and often have more separation anxiety than the child. Some parents are jealous of the closeness that develops between the caregiver and their child. They miss being there for those first steps or other special times. They also feel overstressed by all that they must manage—home, work, childcare, money, meals, and so on.

The director, through in-service training, can make sure the staff is aware of and responsive to parents' feelings. Good communication between teachers and parents is essential to helping parents cope with their child's transition to the program. Discussing how their child is adjusting, asking parents specific questions about their child, and getting the parents to talk about what they like and don't like about the program can all make parents feel more comfortable about leaving their child in the program. Parents of infants and toddlers need information in writing concerning the time they were away from them. This should be given to parents daily and should report when and how much the child ate, when the child was diapered or toileted, and when and for how long the child slept.

Cultural Diversity

The staff must also be aware of and sensitive to ethnic and racial issues and accept both children and their parents into the center (Bollin 1989). You will need to plan for multicultural parent participation (Coleman 1991; Derman-Sparks and A. B. C. Task Force 1989).

11.1 Write up a plan showing what steps you will take each year to ensure that everyone at your center, including children, appreciates the diversity of people of different gender, age, socioeconomic status, ethnic, racial, or religious backgrounds.

11.2 In your group discuss how the director should handle the following situations:

1. The teacher who is Anglo wants children to learn to deal with aggressive behavior by walking away from the aggressor, but an African-American mother complains because she wants her child to learn to defend himself.

2. One of the preschool teachers has several southeast Asian refugee children in her group. They speak no English and she does not know any of the languages spoken by the Hmong.

3. In your center you have several families from a religious group that does not want their children to be involved with the celebration of holidays or birthdays.

With complex family arrangements compounded by separation and divorce, it also is imperative that staff be aware of the legal implications of custody rights as they apply to individual children (Gould 1987). Some custodial parents give very explicit directions that their child is not to be released to the other parent even if the child wishes to go with that parent. Child care workers are sometimes subpoenaed to testify in contested custody proceedings.

Single parents are often overloaded with the demands of job, parenting, and household duties. Some centers provide support groups for single parents or plan social events in which single parents, with or without their children, can participate.

In time parents come to see the center as a positive force in their life as well as their child's. They come to appreciate the center when they are able to work or go to school without undue worry about their child care arrangement. They can also see what exposure to other children and an educational program can do for their young child. Parents can learn good parenting skills from observing trained child care workers. Through their own involvement with the program, they can gain self-esteem.

Communicating with Parents

Information for Parents

Many states require that centers have an annual plan for communicating with parents. Iowa (Department of Human Services 1988) requires that parents have the opportunity to observe their children at times convenient to them and that they be encouraged to work with the program. In centers with more than forty children, parents or parent representatives must make up at least 50 percent of the policy-making board and are charged with initiating ideas for program improvement, assisting in organizing activities for parents, and encouraging parental participation in the program.

Virginia (Department of Social Services 1989) has the following requirements for daily communication with parents:

A. For each infant, the center shall post a daily record which can be easily seen by both the parent and by the staff working with the children. The record shall include the following information: (1) the amount of time the infant slept, (2) the amount of food consumed and the time, (3) a description and the time of bowel movements, and (4) developmental milestones.

B. For toddlers, there shall be daily verbal communication about: (1) daily activities, (2) physical well-being, and (3) developmental milestones. (In some states a daily written report is required.)

Besides the preceding requirements, Oklahoma (Department of Human Services 1987) requires the following:

1. Conferences be held at least once a year and at other times, as needed, to discuss children's progress, accomplishments, and difficulties at home and at the center.
2. Written information on the center's philosophy, program, and policies be provided to new and prospective families.
3. A parent resource area be provided with books, pamphlets, or articles on parenting.
4. Parent meetings with guest speakers or special events be held such as an open house, family potluck dinner, or children's program.
5. Parents be informed of the center's program through a parent's bulletin board or regular newsletter.

Minnesota requires that parents be given the following written information at the time of enrollment (Minnesota Dept. of Human Services 1989, 30–32).

1. Ages and numbers of children the center is licensed to serve.
2. Hours and days of operation.
3. Child care program options the center is licensed to operate, including a description of the program's educational methods and religious, political, or philosophical basis, if any, and how parents may review the center's child care program plan.
4. Center's policy on parent conferences and notification to a parent of a child's intellectual, physical, social, and emotional development.
5. Type and level of liability insurance coverage held by the license holder for the center and for all vehicles owned and operated by the license holder for the transportation of children.
6. Center's policy requiring a health care summary and immunization record of a child.
7. Policies and procedures for the care of children who become sick at the center and parent notification practices for the onset of or exposure to a contagious illness or condition or when there is an emergency or injury requiring medical attention. Also policies for when children can attend who have been ill. How soon after signs of fever, vomiting, when on antibiotics will children be permitted back into school.
8. Center's policies and procedures for administering first aid and sources of care to be used in case of emergencies.
9. Center's policies on the administration of medicine and permission requirement for the administration of ipecac syrup to induce vomiting in cases of suspected poisoning.
10. Procedures for obtaining written parental permission for field trips.
11. Procedures for obtaining written parental permission before each occasion of research, experimental procedure, or public relations activity involving a child.
12. Center's policies on the provision of meals and snacks.
13. Center's behavior guidance policies and procedures.
14. Presence of pets.

15. Center's policy that parents of enrolled children may visit the center any time during the hours of operation.
16. Telephone number of the licensing agent of the state.

Minnesota also requires a preenrollment conference, twice-yearly parent-teacher conferences that are documented in writing in the child's record, and daily written records for an infant or toddler about the child's food intake, elimination, sleeping patterns, and general behavior.

A parent information handbook can be a very useful tool for your program. It can be used at the time of enrollment to acquaint the parents with the program and clarify any misconceptions they may have. It can outline their obligations and responsibilities. This helps avoid many problems that might be caused by inadequate communication later. The handbook can also be sent to social agencies in the community to facilitate referrals to the program (Hatfield and Sheehan 1986).

11.3 Write a parent handbook that will include all the policies you will give to parents when they enroll their child. Check your state's regulations to see what they require. In the absence of stated requirements you may wish to adopt some of those previously listed.

11.4 Examine several parent handbooks put out by different centers. Rate each for comprehensiveness of information, overall design, readability. Which best meets your group's criteria?

The Intake Process/Preenrollment Interview

The procedure used for enrolling a child can be very important in the relationship between the family and the center. This first interview between parents and the director or other staff member can set the tone for their ongoing contacts. A tour of the center and introduction to some of the teachers should take place first. Parents should be made to feel welcome. Their child/children should be included in the intake process if possible. Toys, crayons and paper, and a small table and chair can be set up near the parents. Including children not only gives them a chance to become familiar with the setting in the presence of their parents, but also allows the director or other staff member to observe the child and to make a beginning appraisal of that child's developmental level and personality.

Besides giving parents the center's written policies, the director should also go over them with the parents. A fee agreement must be reached so that parents understand how much they are to pay, when it is due, what other fees such as registration fees or holding fees might be required, and what the penalties are for late payment. The cancellation policy when parents decide to remove their child from the program must be explained. Parents must also know their child's schedule and what they will need to bring in the way of personal items (blanket, extra clothing, formula, etc.). From the parent the director will get a developmental and social history of the child, a general impression of how the child might react in a group setting, how discipline is handled at home, and how the parent feels about placing the child in the program. She may then give the parent the registration form to fill out. If she thinks they might have difficulty in completing the form, she can fill it in for them as the discussion goes on.

The enrollment packet usually contains many forms. Included will be permission forms for field trips, emergency treatment, picture taking, administering medicine, and so on. There will also be a health form that the family's physician will complete. The registration form will have information about the child's preferences in food, people, and toys. It might contain questions about their fears and reactions to stress. Any program would want names, addresses, and phone numbers to contact if parents could not be reached in an emergency.

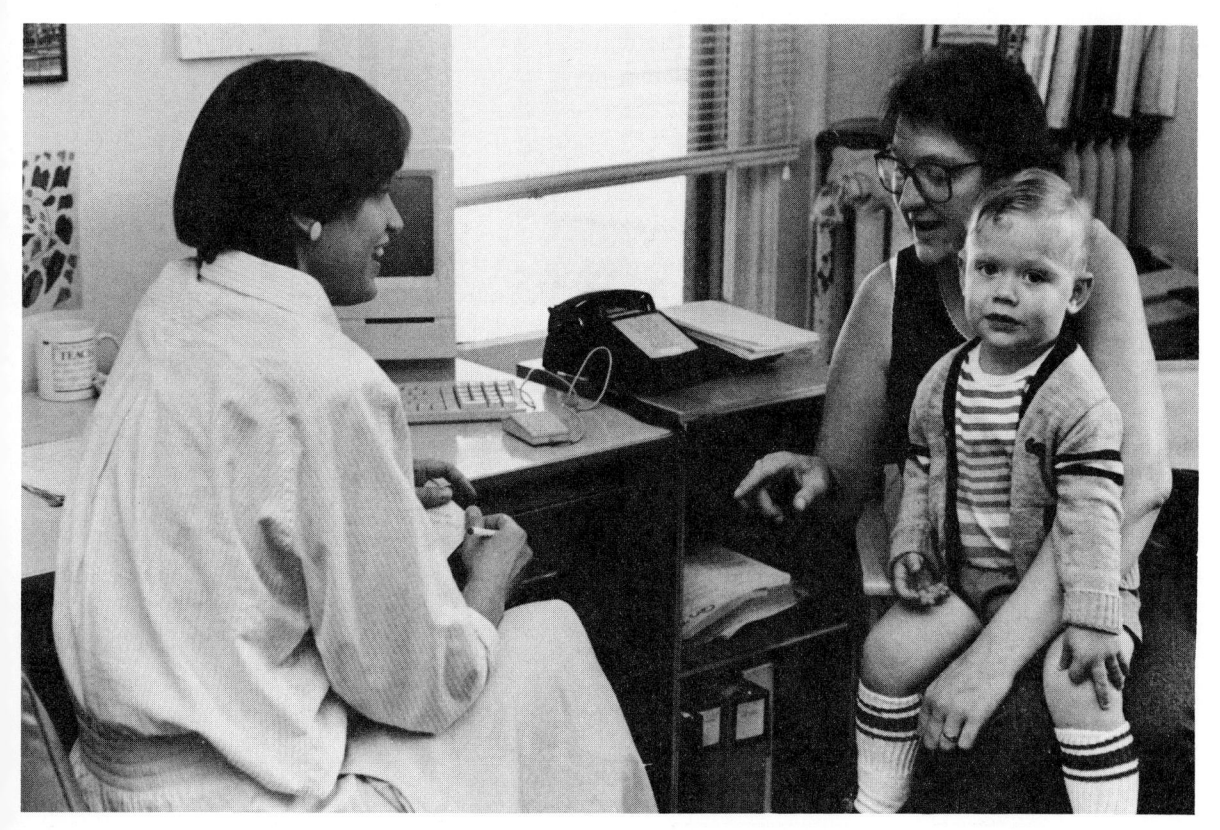

The director must make certain this mother understands the center's policies and feels comfortable leaving her son there. Photo by Rob Skelnar

Once the child is enrolled, the tuition paid, and the parents have been given the information they will need, the director will need to take some time to show the parents the room where their child will be. The parents should be introduced to the child's teacher/teachers. The director may have to take over for the teacher for a few minutes so he or she can spend some time talking to the parents about their child and what they can expect from the program.

Parent-Teacher Conferences

Besides daily communication between the child's caregiver and the parent that takes place when the child is brought in to the center in the morning or when the child is picked up in the afternoon, the teaching staff is mandated in most states to have a formal conference with parents. For preschool and school-age children, this is scheduled twice a year. For infants and toddlers, this occurs once a month. The purpose of these conferences is to enable both parent and caregiver to share information about the child so that they can prevent or remedy any problems for the child and work together to help the child.

Before the conference takes place the teacher should have the opportunity to make several behavioral observations of the child, noting the way he or she relates to adults and other children, what activities he or she enjoys or avoids, his or her physical abilities, and his or her general emotional tone. Samples of art or written work, anecdotal accounts of play behaviors, tape recordings or videotapes of the child's interaction and verbal exchange with others, and checklists of intellectual tasks completed are some ways of documenting each child's developmental progress.

Parents should be encouraged to contribute too. Asking questions about what kinds of behaviors parents are seeing at home, what problems they are encountering, what their child likes or doesn't like about the center, and what activities or discipline works best for this child is an effective way to keep the conference focused on the child. Teachers will also want to be informed about family

Working with Parents

problems or traumas that may be affecting the child's behavior. Parents should be free to ask their own questions of the teacher and given pencil and paper if they wish to take notes.

Besides talking about their child many parents will welcome an opportunity to discuss their own problems with a sympathetic adult. Teaching staff may not feel comfortable doing this and may want to refer the parent to the social worker or director for further counseling or referral to another agency. Setting a time limit for parent-teacher conferences and sticking to it is a good practice for teachers with busy schedules and many parent conference appointments. Morrison (1988) has suggested that teachers be on time and start on time, talk so parents can understand what is said, give parents helpful parenting suggestions, solicit and consider parents' feelings and ideas, and summarize what has been discussed to bring closure to the conference. He also advised that following up on what was decided is essential; otherwise, conferences are a waste of everyone's time.

Preparing for and conducting parent-teacher conferences is a time-consuming process. Providing a substitute or some other way of allowing staff to have compensatory time off can help them see that this is a necessary and important part of their job.

11.5 Write a letter to parents that a teacher might send inviting the parents to a conference concerning their child's progress.

11.6 Write up a sample form for teachers to use when conferring with parents about their child's intellectual, physical, social, and emotional development. Give a copy to the child's parents and keep one for the child's file.

11.7 If your center will serve infants and toddlers, compose a sheet that will be given to parents daily noting times and amounts of food eaten, a record of eliminations, time spent napping, and any other information your group deems important.

Parent Meetings

Parent meetings that include children are always better attended than meetings with parents alone. Parents will come to watch their children perform even if they only sing a few songs. If invited, grandparents, close friends, and neighbors will come too. If the director or teaching staff needs to meet with the parents only, child care should be provided.

11.8 Plan an evening meeting as an orientation for new and returning families in the early fall. If your center is very large, you may want to do it room by room or have one group come at a time. Think about how many people will be involved. What will be the purpose of this meeting? What time will it be? How long will it last? Will children be included? Will you serve refreshments? Discuss these questions in your group.

11.9 Make a schedule of other events during the year that will include parents. How will parents be involved in the planning?

Other Ways to Involve Parents

These suggestions are gathered from several different child care programs and are meant only to give you a few ideas of the many ways the director and staff can include parents in the everyday operation of a child care center.

1. Set up a sign-in book where either parents or teachers can leave messages to each other.

2. Send out a biweekly or monthly newsletter announcing upcoming events, giving profiles of staff members, discussing specific concepts the children will be learning, and suggesting happenings in the community that parents and children might be interested in attending.

3. Encourage teachers to keep in daily contact with parents when they drop off or pick up their child. Ask staff to write notes, telephone, or send tapes to those parents who cannot make it to the center on a regular basis.

4. Stagger your schedule so that you can be there early some days and stay late on others. This enables you to keep in contact with all families.

5. Involve parents as volunteers in the program. You or someone you designate can send out a letter to all parents asking for their help. When they do volunteer, have a brief handbook on how they should interact with the children. Also have a written assignment for what activities you expect them to carry out while they are there. Follow up with them to see how it went. Give them recognition. A special "Thank you" note, a mention in the newsletter, or a dinner for all volunteers once a year are some ways you can express your appreciation.

6. Invite parents to serve on your policy board. If several are interested, call a meeting of the parents or set up some balloting process so they can vote for their own representatives.

7. Have an area or room that is just for parents. Include comfortable seating and a coffee and/or tea pot. Have books, videos, and magazines that deal with parenting issues. Have a bulletin board that parents can use to advertise their own events.

8. Have dinners. These can be potlucks or prepared meals that parents buy. Working parents are always delighted when they can feed their family inexpensively and have fun with their children and other families.

9. Facilitate parents' getting to know each other. Some of the most lasting friendships between children and between parents start at the child care center. Introduce them to each other. Supply name tags at meetings. Encourage ride-sharing.

10. Make home visits. Although this is very time consuming and may be impossible to do for all families, there is no better way to get to know the child and his or her family. Encourage teachers to do this especially with children who are having difficulty adjusting to the center. Give compensatory time off or overtime for these efforts.

11. Have regularly scheduled parent conferences. See that teachers get help or a substitute while they are conducting these.

12. As the director, you can be a resource of great importance to parents. Be sensitive to the needs of working parents. Schedule events at their convenience. Also be aware of the special problems of single parents. Be certain you know who has custody in divorce cases. Work with the staff to avoid any discrimination of handicapped or culturally different parents.

13. Be available to talk with parents. Give them support for their parenting role. Be positive about their child. Tell them about the good things their child has done as well as mentioning any problems he or she might be having.

11.10 In your group write down at least two more ways the child care center director and staff can involve parents.

A Social/Family Worker

If your center enrolls a large number of children, you may be able to hire on a part-time or full-time basis a social worker, parent educator, or family specialist whose main job would be to work with parents. This person could handle the intake process and give each new family the information they might need to see if the program meets their needs and those of their child. She or he would monitor the transition process between home and center for each child and help the parents adjust to a new schedule.

The social worker could work with parents' income statements to determine fees. If state sliding fee scales or public money is available to parents, the social worker could help parents apply for these. Someone in this position could arrange support groups for parents experiencing problems such as divorce, addictions, chronic illness, etc.

The social worker could also be familiar with other agencies in the community that serve families. Many family professionals within the community can provide therapy and support beyond what the center is able to offer (Coleman 1991). She or he could make information available to parents and assist them in receiving services by making referrals.

If the program cannot afford to hire someone just to work with families, this responsibility is the director's or someone she appoints from her staff. In some centers the social worker role is carried out by the assistant director.

Summary

Working with parents to make them comfortable about leaving their child at the center is an important part of the director's role. She is responsible for making her staff sensitive and responsive to parental input. She also must see that effective communication is established and maintained between the center and families. Suggestions for ways to involve parents are given. The social/family worker position is examined.

References

Berger, E. H. 1987. *Parents as partners in education: The school and home working together.* Columbus, OH: Merrill.

Bollin, G. G. 1989. Ethnic differences in attitudes towards discipline among day care providers: Implications for training. *Child & Youth Care Quarterly* 18: 111–117.

Coleman, M. 1991. Planning for the changing nature of family life in schools for young children. *Young Children* 46(4): 15–20.

Derman-Sparks, L., and A. B. C. Task Force. 1989. *Anti-bias curriculum: Tools for empowering young children.* Washington, DC: NAEYC.

Gould, N. P. 1987. Legal implications of divorce and custody battles for day care administrators. *Day Care and Early Education* 15: 14–17.

Hatfield, L. M., and S. P. Sheehan. 1986. Parent information manual: A vital link between home and school. *Child Care Information Exchange* 49: 29–31.

Iowa Department of Human Services. 1988. *Child day care centers and preschools licensing standards and procedures.* (SS-0711). Des Moines, IA: Department of Human Services.

Lazar, I., R. Darlington, H. Murray, J. Royce, and A. Snipper. 1982. Lasting effects of early education: A report from the Consortium for Longitudinal Studies. *Monographs of the Society for Research in Child Development* 47(2–3, No. 195).

Leavitt, R. L., and B. K. Eheart. 1985. *Toddler day care: A guide to responsive caregiving.* Lexington, MA: Lexington Books.

Minnesota Department of Human Services. 1989. *Child care centers.* (Chapter 9503). St. Paul, MN: Department of Human Services.

Morrison, G. S. 1988. *Education and development of infants, toddlers, and preschoolers.* Glenview, IL: Scott, Foresman Company.

Oklahoma Department of Human Services. 1987. *Requirements for day care centers.* (Pub. No. 84–08). Oklahoma City, OK: Department of Human Services.

Sale, J. 1984. Why I'm involved with parent involvement. *Child Care Information Exchange* (Dec.): 25–27.

Umansky, W. 1983. On families and the re-valuing of childhood. *Childhood Education* 59: 260–266.

Virginia Department of Social Services. 1989. *Minimum standards for licensed child care centers.* (032–05–009/8). Richmond, VA: Department of Human Services.

11.1

What steps will you take each year to ensure that everyone at your center, including children, appreciates the diversity of people of different gender, age, socioeconomic status, ethnic, racial, or religious backgrounds?

1.

2.

3.

4.

5.

6.

7.

8.

11.2

How should a director handle the following situations?

1. Teacher and parent want child to learn different ways of dealing with aggression.

2. The teacher and Hmong children in the classroom have no common language.

3. Several families do not want their children to participate in holiday or birthday celebrations.

11.3

Write a parent handbook after first checking with your state's licensing requirements about information to be given to parents.

Use this page for a rough draft.

11.4

Examine several parent handbooks put out by different centers. Rate them (1 = Poor 6 = Excellent)

Center's Name	Comprehensiveness of Information	Overall Design	Readability

Which best meets your group's criteria?

11.5

Write a letter to parents inviting them to a conference with the teacher about their child's progress.

11.6

Prepare a form for teachers to use when conferring with parents about their child's intellectual, physical, social, and emotional development.

11.7

Compose a daily information sheet that will be given to parents of infants and toddlers noting times and amounts of food eaten, a record of eliminations, and time spent napping. Are there other items your group wishes to include?

11.8

Plan an evening "orientation" meeting for parents. What will be the purpose of this meeting? Make a schedule for what will happen. How many people will be involved? Will children be included? Will you serve refreshments?

11.9

Make a schedule of other events during the year that will include parents. How will parents be involved in the planning?

11.10

In your group write down at least two more ways the child care center director and staff can involve parents.

12

MARKETING YOUR PROGRAM

Chapter Outline

Marketing suggestions

Summary

References

Assignments

12.1 Write a press release.

12.2 Write a telephone script.

12.3 Plan an Open House for prospective parents.

12.4 Plan a breakfast meeting for businesspeople.

12.5 Discuss two other marketing strategies your center could use.

12.6 Choose the one marketing idea that your group thinks would work best for your community.

Once you have your program set up and operating it is crucial that you get children enrolled and that you be able to retain them. In some communities this is no problem because there is such a need for child care that many families are ready and eager for the services you provide. In others the competition is stiff and many programs are vying for the same families. You must be very clear about what your program has to offer them. You should also distinguish what makes your program unique and emphasize that in your advertising (Kingsbury, Vogler, and Benero 1990). For example, if your teachers are all certified in early childhood education, you might include that information in your advertising. Another center might focus on its well-equipped playground or the fact that a physician comes to the center once a month to examine infants and toddlers.

However, it is the kind of personal attention that you give to children and parents and what they see when they enter the center's doors that will get them to enroll. The teaching and support staff members must all be aware of the important role they play through their daily contact with parents and children in keeping families satisfied with the services they get at the center.

Marketing Suggestions

The following list of marketing suggestions was made by Roger Neugebauer, editor of *Child Care Information Exchange,* at a Minnesota Association for the Education of Young Children fall conference in Minneapolis several years ago and is used with permission. That journal frequently has a column with tested ideas for helping make the public more aware of the child care services available.*

1. Be attentive to your current clients/families. Parents who are satisfied with your program will tell their friends and relatives. Word-of-mouth publicity is the best public relations.

2. Stimulate complaints and deal with them. People who are unhappy and don't tell you can spread negative comments about your program. Make it easy for them to tell you. Periodically question parents about how they feel. Have a suggestion box. Have a parent representative call every parent and bring back any concerns parents have. Then, take care of the trouble. Write all parents a letter explaining the complaint and what you have done to fix it or why you can't make the changes needed to eliminate the complaint.

3. Encourage positive feedback too. Encourage parents to tell others about your center. Give rewards for referrals. (Some programs give a week's free tuition for bringing another family in.)

4. As the director, explore every opportunity for being the expert in child development concerns. Write your own column in the newspaper. Director and staff should get involved in child advocacy issues in their community or state. Offer workshops and seminars on hot topics to parents and the public.

5. Get the newspapers to write an article about your center. Write letters to the editor. Have special events and ask the newspaper to send a photographer. Write up news releases about special programs at your center and mail them out to the radio, television, and newspapers in your town or region. Find out who on their staffs covers children's issues or education and let them know when you will be doing something newsworthy. Never hound them for publicity. (Some successful news stories for the campus preschool I [the author] direct include front-page pictures of children taping up their artwork in a downtown building as part of a celebration of Week of the Young Child, a story and picture of children interacting with elderly residents of a nursing home, and an article in which director, teacher, and parents were interviewed about their year-long emphasis on the Anti-Bias Curriculum. This was followed up by an unsolicited editorial on the need for all to be aware of cultural diversity.)

---

*Reprinted with permission of Exchange Press, Inc. Publisher of *Child Care Information Exchange* (a bi-monthly management magazine for owner and directors), P.O. Box 2890, Redmond, WA 98073–9977.

6. Keep all your public statements simple and focused on the message you want to convey. Identify what makes your program unique and concentrate on that as a selling point.

7. Be consistent. Use the same logo or symbol on all your stationery, posters, T-shirts. The effect is cumulative.

8. Make your printed materials attractive. Use good quality paper. Have your printing professionally done. Neugebauer suggested using line drawings instead of photos on brochures. "Only use photos if they are fantastic."

9. Make a good first impression by training your staff to answer the phone. Give them a procedure (script) to follow. They should all know the hours, the fees charged, and the key selling points of your program. Have them make an appointment for the family to come and visit your center. Follow up phone calls by mailing out information.

10. Make visitors feel welcome. Greet them by name. Have someone there to talk to them if you can't be there yourself. Give them a tour of the center. Don't overwhelm them with information. Introduce them to teachers and let them talk to them if possible. Give them a little time to observe in the classroom where their child might be enrolled. When the tour is over, talk to them about how they felt about what they saw. Talk about their own child. Ask them if they would like to enroll their child.

11. Schedule a visiting day once a week. Take two or three sets of visitors around together. This minimizes interrupting the classrooms and allows you to give your talk to several families at a time. At the end of the visit, ask parents how they felt about what they saw. If they react favorably, ask them directly if they wish to enroll their child.

2.1 Write up a press release announcing one of the following events: (1) one of your teachers is going to make a presentation about "art for toddlers" at a state early childhood conference, (2) the children in your program are going to ride the train to a city thirty miles away, (3) a father is coming in to work with the children on a large wood sculpture, or (4) a mother from West Africa is going to make Ground Nut Stew with the children.

2.2 Write a script for staff members to use when prospective clients telephone and want to know how to enroll their child.

An Open House for prospective parents is a good way also to talk to many people at one time (Scirra and Dorsey 1990). The center should be arranged as it would be for children. All the staff and board members should be invited so they can interact with individual parents. The program should be carefully planned. This is an excellent way to launch a new program.

2.3 In your group plan an Open House for prospective parents. What materials will you have available for them to look at? What time of day will it be held? What will be included in your talk to the group? Will refreshments be served? Will child care be provided?

2.4 Once you are open and operating you may still find that your program is not very well known in the community. Plan a breakfast meeting and invite local businesspeople. What do you want to happen at this meeting? How can you ensure that your goals will be met?

This mother and daughter attend an Open House to find out more about the program. *Photo by Steve Hermann*

The child care resource and referral agency in your region can also let parents know that you have openings. Be certain that your program is enrolled and keep your information up-to-date. (This agency generally has a computerized service that matches families looking for certain types of care with community providers who offer the services they want.)

12.5 Think of at least two other ways your center could reach potential clients. Discuss them in your group. Share your ideas with other groups in your class.

12.6 Which idea does your group think would be the most effective way to reach clients in your community?

Summary

This chapter offered several field-tested ideas that have proven effective for making the public more aware of your center and the services it has to offer to families.

References

Kingsbury, D. F., S. K. Vogler, and C. Benero. 1990. *The everyday guide to opening and operating a child care center.* Denver, CO: Vade Mecum Press.

Neugebauer, R. *Marketing your program: Keys to success.* Presentation given at the MnAEYC Fall Conference, Minneapolis, MN.

Sciarra, D. J., and A. G. Dorsey. 1990. *Developing and administering a child care center.* 2d ed. Albany, NY: Delmar.

12.1

Write a press release announcing one of the following events:

1. One of your teachers is going to make a presentation about "art for toddlers" at a state early childhood conference.

2. The children in your program are going to ride the train to a city thirty miles away.

3. A father is coming in to work with the children on a large wood sculpture.

4. A mother from West Africa is going to make Ground Nut Stew with the children.

12.2

Write a script for staff members to use when prospective clients telephone and want to know how to enroll their child.

12.3

Plan an Open House for prospective parents. What materials will you have available for them? What time of day will it be held? What will be included in your talk to the group? Will refreshments be served? Will child care be provided?

12.4

Plan a breakfast meeting for community businesspeople. What do you want to happen at this meeting? How can you ensure that your goals are met?

Goals for this meeting:

1.

2.

3.

How you will ensure that your goals are met:

1.

2.

3.

4.

How you will evaluate your meeting to see if it was successful:

1.

2.

3.

12.5

Think of at least two other ways your center could reach potential clients. Discuss them in your group. Share your ideas with other groups in your class.

12.6

Which idea does your group think would be the most effective way to reach clients in your community?

Why?

13

EVALUATION IN CHILD CARE PROGRAMS

Chapter Outline

The use of evaluation in child care programs

Types of evaluation commonly used in child care programs

Summary

References

Assignments

13.1 Review goals and write specific objectives.

13.2 Choose one aspect of accreditation and develop evaluation tools to measure your center's progress.

13.3 Review another group's evaluation materials.

13.4 Compare your checklist with the items in *Accreditation Criteria and Procedures* (NAEYC 1984). Discuss how you might change your checklist.

13.5 Write a form for parents to use in evaluating one aspect of your program.

The Use of Evaluation in Child Care Programs

Summative and Formative Evaluation

Evaluation in child care programs means gathering information about the processes and outcomes to aid in decision making. The focus of the evaluation can vary. It can center on the functioning of the entire program or focus on one specific part of the program. Johnson (1987) differentiated between *summative* and *formative* evaluation in early childhood programs. Summative evaluation looks at the overall effectiveness of the program or instruction and is usually based on children's test results, observations of children's behaviors, social indicators such as attendance records, retention in grade, or assignment to special education classes. Formative or process evaluation assesses the effectiveness of the program while it is in progress in order to improve the methods used. In general less formal day to-day observations and records of activities or child progress are used.

Finding a Focus for Evaluation

In a complex social institution such as a child care center, endless areas of operation require evaluation. The director and staff are limited, however, by the amount of time, money, and expertise available to carry out the evaluations. Evaluation topics and methods must be chosen carefully to make the best use of resources at the center's disposal. The following are just a few examples of different aspects of the program that *could* be evaluated: (1) the physical environment of each classroom could be examined to see if it meets the space needs of the children and staff, (2) the teacher's ability to plan and carry out a developmentally appropriate curriculum with young children, or (3) the degree to which meal preparation follows the guidelines advocated by the state and local health authorities. Looking at the children in the program to see how they are progressing in several different spheres by using teachers' checklists or rating scales would be valuable in planning the curriculum (Cherry, Harkness, and Kuzma 1987; Hendrick 1990). Evaluating a staff member's effectiveness as a teacher to acknowledge his or her accomplishments and motivate further achievements is part of the director's responsibility (Click and Click 1990; Storm 1985) Whatever the focus, the data gathered will help the administrator, board members, and/or staff make judgments about the way things are being done and institute changes where necessary. The objective is to improve the operations of the center so services to children and families can be better.

The Evaluation Process

According to Kostelnik (1987) the evaluation process consists of six steps:

1. Formulating meaningful evaluation questions
2. Designing a means for gathering the information necessary to answer the evaluation questions
3. Collecting relevant data
4. Analyzing the data
5. Reporting the findings to the appropriate parties
6. Using the information gained to determine a course of action

Types of Evaluation Commonly Used in Child Care Programs

Group Evaluation

The *Early Childhood Environment Rating Scale* (Harms and Clifford 1980) and the *Infant/Toddler Environment Rating Scale* (Harms, Cryer, and Clifford 1990) have been shown to be useful self-evaluation tools to use with one classroom or one group of children. Both instruments examine several different areas: personal care routines, furnishings and display, language/reasoning experiences, fine and gross motor activities, creative activities, social development, and adult needs. Evidence from field testing showed that center staff were able and willing to make the observations needed and that centers initiated many improvements in their programs as a result of using the rating scales (Kontos and Stevens 1985).

Program Evaluation

An assessment process may be used to measure the quality of the entire program. According to Ware, Olmsted, and Newell (1976), program evaluation attempts to answer several questions. These include:

1. What are the effects of the program and how does it compare with other programs?
2. How well does the program compare to established standards (criteria)?
3. Do the activities correspond to the objectives?
4. Is the program worth the cost?

Each program establishes goals and objectives. The evaluation process is an effort to see if the program is meeting these stated ends and/or monitoring the progress that has been made toward the desired outcomes.

For example, one of your goals might be to provide a homelike setting. Under this goal you might list some very clear objectives that will enable you to meet this goal. For instance, three things that you might agree upon that would make each room resemble the child's home would be: (1) to have both a male and a female caregiver in each room, (2) to group children in family units ranging in age from infants to school-age, and (3) to make the environment soft and cozy by providing couches, pillows, curtains, and stuffed animals.

Once your group has decided on written goals and how they will be reached, it becomes fairly easy to devise a way to show whether progress is being made in meeting them. Either you have or have not been able to find qualified male and female teachers for your center. Perhaps your teachers report that family grouping is working well except for the school-age children. Integrating them into existing groups when they come in from school may be a problem that needs some creative solutions. One can count the number of pillows, couches, or other soft items that have been added to the classrooms.

3.1 Review the goals you made earlier for your program. These are usually written in very general terms. Rewrite one or two of them using specific, behavioral objectives. Discuss how you will know when you are meeting one or more of your goals. What objective documentation will you need to show to others that you are making progress toward meeting this goal?

After the scope of the evaluation has been discussed and decisions have been made about the focus or focuses, then the process must be set up for getting the information. "Who is going to do what by

A flower shop offers many opportunities for dramatic play. Setting up different learning centers is part of a good curriculum. *Photo by Steve Hermann*

when, as evidenced by what?" (Ware, Olmsted, and Newell 1976, 149). Identify the staff or board member responsible for collecting the data. Set a date by which time all the necessary material will be collected. Determine how the objective will be measured. Decide the format to be used in reporting the results.

Meeting Licensing Requirements

Most states have some kind of licensing process that they institute to ensure that out-of-the-home care for young children meets minimum standards. In general the state gets input from providers and parents in determining the requirements.

The state sends out information forms that must be completed, submitted, and reviewed before a licensing consultant makes an on-site visit. The consultant then observes the program, examines staff and children's records, inspects the premises, goes over logs of accidents, fire drills, and so on, and clarifies policies and procedures with the director. The licenser then notes any violations and discusses how they can be corrected. The visit is followed with a written list of conditions that must be rectified by a certain time. Failure to make the recommended improvements can result in sanctions against the center/provider.

The states' regulation of all types of child care is strongly endorsed by the National Association for the Education of Young Children as being beneficial in ensuring that centers, family day care, and group homes meet a certain basic minimum quality (NAEYC 1987). They also recommend that public school and church-sponsored programs be required to meet the same or higher standards.

Accreditation

The National Association for the Education of Young Children has set up an accreditation process that looks at all aspects of early childhood programs (NAEYC 1984). It includes a self-study component, a written report to the National Academy of Early Childhood Programs, and a validation visit by a trained early childhood professional to verify the accuracy of the program description. Then a three-member commission considers all the components of the written report and the validator's report and either grants or defers accreditation. Although this accreditation is voluntary and needs to be renewed every three years, this process is seen as one that promotes and encourages improvement in each of the programs that undergoes this examination.

Each center needs to engage in ongoing and systematic evaluation to maintain and improve the program. This means identifying the center's strengths as well as the areas where there are weaknesses. Not only the director, but also staff, parents, board members, and others outside the program should be involved.

The NAEYC accreditation process has delineated criteria for the following aspects of high-quality early childhood programs:

A. Interactions among staff and children

B. Curriculum

C. Staff-parent interaction

D. Staff qualifications and development

E. Administration

F. Staffing

G. Physical environment

H. Health and safety

I. Nutrition and food service

J. Evaluation

A follow-up study of seventy-eight programs one year after they were accredited showed that nearly all had met the recommendations of the Academy either fully or in part (Bredekamp and Berby 1987). Most programs noted greater parent involvement and better relationships with families since the assessment process.

Although the Academy's self-study materials include many useful evaluation tools, you and those you work with can develop materials that are specific to your program and your unique situation.

3.2 Before looking at the criteria that the Academy has proposed, decide which aspects of your program you want to examine more closely. If the group is large enough, divide up all the aspects so each group is working on only one or two. Devise a checklist that you could use to determine if your center is operating effectively in this area.

3.3 After your group has devised an evaluation tool for at least one aspect of the program, exchange with another group. Analyze what they have done. What have they left out? What suggestions would you have for improving the instrument? If groups work on different evaluation materials, you will end up with material that will be useful in monitoring many parts of your center's program.

3.4 If you do not already have it, send for copies of *Accreditation Criteria and Procedures* (NAEYC 1984). Compare the instruments you have created with the items they have developed.

13.5 Parents are a vital source of information about the program. Storm (1985) felt that it was useful to survey parents several times during a year focusing on one or two issues at a time. Design a questionnaire for parents to elicit their attitudes about the way they are kept aware of what is happening at the center. Ask for suggestions for improving communications between staff and them. Leave room for other comments beyond the questions you ask. If possible, make this questionnaire no more than one page and easy to answer. What process will you set up to ensure that the respondents remain anonymous and that you get a good return?

Summary

Child care centers need to find and use methods for evaluating their programs. Deciding whether it will be focused on individual performance, group functioning, or the status of the entire center is a first step. Establishing the focus of the evaluation, who will carry it out, what kind of data will be collected, and how it will be presented are next. All centers will have to supply some kind of documentation of what they are doing for licensing or accreditation purposes.

References

Bredekamp, S., and J. Berby. 1987. Maintaining quality: Accredited programs one year later. *Young Children* 43: 13–15.

Cherry, C., B. Harkness, and K. Kuzma. 1987. *Nursery school and day care center management guide.* 2d ed. Belmont, CA: David S. Lake Publishers.

Click, P. M., and D. W. Click. 1990. *Administration of schools for young children.* 3d ed. Albany, NY: Delmar.

Harms, T., and R. M. Clifford. 1980. *The early childhood environment rating scale.* New York: Teachers College Press.

Harms, T., D. Cryer, and R. M. Clifford. 1990. *Infant/toddler environment rating scale.* New York: Teachers College Press.

Hendrick, J. 1990. *Total learning: Developmental curriculum for the young child.* 3d ed. Columbus, OH: Merrill.

Johnson, J. E. 1987. Evaluation in early childhood education. In *Approaches to early childhood education*, ed. J. L. Roopnarine and J. E. Johnson. Columbus, OH: Merrill.

Kontos, S., and R. Stevens. 1985. High quality child care: Does your center measure up? *Young Children* 40: 5–9.

Kostelnik, M. 1987. Program evaluation: How to ask the right questions. *Child Care Information Exchange* 56: 3–8.

National Association for the Education of Young Children. 1984. *Accreditation criteria and procedures of the National Academy of Early Childhood Programs.* Washington, DC: NAEYC.

———. 1987. NAEYC position statement on licensing and other forms of regulation of early childhood programs in centers and family day care homes. *Young Children* 42: 64–68.

Storm, S. 1985. *The human side of child care administration: A how-to manual.* Washington, DC: NAEYC.

Ware, W. B., P. P. Olmsted, and J. M. Newell. 1976. Designing an evaluation for home-school programs. In *Building effective home-school relationships*, 149–175. ed. I. J. Gordon and W. F. Breivogel. Boston: Allyn and Bacon.

13.1

Choose a goal that you have for your program. Write it here.

1. Rewrite this goal using specific behavioral objectives.

2. How will you know when you are meeting one or more of your goals?

3. What objective documentation will you need to show to others that you are making progress toward meeting this goal?

13.2

Decide which aspects of your program you want to examine more closely. Divide the work so that each group is working on only one or two areas. Devise a checklist that you could use to determine if your center is operating effectively on this aspect.

13.3

Exchange your checklist with another group. Analyze what they have done answering the following questions:

1. What are the good points of the evaluation tool they devised?

2. What have they left out?

3. What suggestions do you have for improving their checklist?

13.4

If you have copies of the *Accreditation Criteria and Procedures* (NAEYC 1984), compare it with your evaluation checklist on the same aspect.

1. What items were similar?

2. How would you change your checklist after comparing the two instruments?

13.5

Design a questionnaire for parents focusing on communication between the center and parents.
Make this one page with easy-to-answer questions. Elicit their suggestions for ways to improve their awareness about what is happening at the center.

1. How will you introduce the questionnaire?

2. What questions will you ask?

3. How will you ensure that the respondents remain anonymous?

4. How will you guarantee that most parents will fill out and return the questionnaire?

A

STATE LICENSING AND CERTIFICATION AGENCIES

(Taken from Decker, C. A. & Decker, J. R. (1992). Planning and administering early childhood programs (fifth ed.). Columbus, OH: Merrill. Reprinted with permission of Merrill, an imprint of Macmillan Publishing Company.)

State	State Department Responsible For Licensing	State Department Responsible For Certification
Alabama	**Department of Human Resources** Office of Day-Care & Child Development G. Gordon Persons Building 50 Ripley Street Montgomery, AL 36130	**Department of Education** State Office Building Montgomery, AL 36130
Alaska	**Department of Health and Social Services** Division of Family and Youth Services P.O. Box H-05 Juneau, AK 99811	**Department of Education** Pouch F Juneau, AK 99811
Arizona	**Department of Economic Security** Box 6123 Phoenix, AZ 85005	**Department of Education** 1535 West Jefferson Street Phoenix, AZ 85007
Arkansas	**Department of Human Services** Division of Children & Family Child Care Licensing P.O. Box 1437, Slot 720 Little Rock, AR 72203	**Department of Education** #4 Capitol Mall, Room 107–B Little Rock, AR 72201
California	**Department of Social Services** Children's Day Care Bureau 3701 Branch Center Road Sacramento, CA 95812 Office of Child Development 1500 5th Street, 3rd Floor Sacramento, CA 95814	**Commission on Teacher Credentialing** P.O. Box 944270 Sacramento, CA 95244

225

Colorado	**Department of Social Services** 1575 Sherman Street Denver, CO 80203	**Department of Education** 201 East Colfax Ave. Denver, CO 80203
Connecticut	**Department of Children and Youth Services** 170 Sigourney Street Hartford, CT 06105	**Department of Education** Box 2219 Hartford, CT 06145
Delaware	**Child Support Office** Office of Secretary 1901 Dupont Hwy. New Castle, DE 19720	**Department of Public Instruction** The Townsend Building P.O. Box 1402 Dover, DE 19903
Florida	**Department of Health and Rehabilitative Services** Family Support Services 1317 Winewood Blvd. Tallahassee, FL 32301	**Bureau of Teacher Education and Certification** State Department of Education Tallahassee, FL 32399
Georgia	**Department of Human Resources** Room 606 Atlanta, GA 30309	**Department of Education** Twin Towers East Atlanta, GA 30334
Hawaii	**Department of Social Services and Housing** P.O. 339 Honolulu, HI 96809	**Department of Education** P.O. Box 2360 Honolulu, HI 96804
Idaho	**Department of Health and Welfare** Division of Field Operations 4355 Emerald Boise, ID 83706	**State Department of Education** Boise, ID 82720
Illinois	**Department of Children and Family Services** 406 East Monroe Springfield, IL 62701	**State Board of Education** 100 N. First Street Springfield, IL 62777
Indiana	**Department of Public Welfare** Child Welfare/Social Services Division 141 South Meridian Street, 6th Floor Indianapolis, IN 46225	**Department of Education** State House, Room 229 Indianapolis, IN 46204
Iowa	**Department of Human Services** Hoover State Office Building Des Moines, IA 50319	**Department of Public Instruction** Grimes State Office Building Des Moines, IA 50319
Kansas	**Department of Health and Environment** Bureau of Adult & Child Care 900 Southwest Jackson Topeka, KS 66612	**Department of Education** 120 E. 10th Street Topeka, KS 66612

Kentucky	**Cabinet for Human Resources** Office of Inspector General 275 East Main Frankfort, KY 40621	**Department of Education** Capital Plaza Frankfort, KY 40621
Louisiana	**Department of Health & Hospitals** Bureau of Health Services Financing Health Standards Section P.O. Box 3767 Baton Rouge, LA 70821	**Department of Education** P.O. Box 94064 Baton Rouge, LA 70804
Maine	**Department of Human Services** State House, Station No. 11 Augusta, ME 04333	**State Department of Education** State House, Station No. 23 Augusta, ME 04333
Maryland	**Office of Child Care Licensing and Regulation** 311 West Saratoga Street Baltimore, MD 21201	**Department of Education** 200 West Baltimore Street Baltimore, MD 21201
Massachusetts	**Office of Children** 10 West Street Boston, MA 02111	**Department of Education** 1385 Hancock Street Quincy, MA 02169
Michigan	**Department of Social Services** 300 South Capitol Ave. P.O. Box 30037 Lansing, MI 48909	**Department of Education** P.O. Box 30008 Lansing, MI 48909
Minnesota	**Department of Human Resources** 1060 East Kellogg St. Paul, MN 55101	**Department of Education** 550 Cedar Street St. Paul, MN 55101
Mississippi	**State Department of Health** P.O. Box 1700 Jackson, MS 39205	**State Department of Education** P.O. Box 771 Jackson, MS 39205
Missouri	**Department of Social Services** Division of Family Services P.O. Box 88, Broadway Building Jefferson City, MO 65102	**Department of Elementary and Secondary Education** P. O. Box 480 Jefferson City, MO 65102
Montana	**Department of Family Services** P.O. Box 8005 Helena, MT 59604	**Office of Public Instruction** State Capitol Helena, MT 59620
Nebraska	**Department of Social Services** 301 Centennial Mall South Box 95026 Lincoln, NE 68509	**Department of Education** 301 Centennial Mall South Box 94987 Lincoln, NE 68509
Nevada	**Bureau of Services for Child Care** 505 E. King Street, Room 606 Carson City, NV 87710	**State Department of Education** Capital Complex Carson City, NV 89710

New Hampshire	**Department of Public Health Services** Bureau of Child Care Standards & Licensing Health and State Building Hazen Drive Concord, NH 03301	**State Department of Education** State Office Park South 101 Pleasant Street Concord, NH 03301
New Jersey	**Department of Human Services** Division of Youth and Family Services Princess Road, Bldg. 9–F—CN 717 Lawrenceville, NJ 08648	**Department of Education** 225 West State Street—CN 503 Trenton, NJ 08625
New Mexico	**Health & Environment Department** P.O. Box 068 Santa Fe, NM 87504	**State Department of Education** Education Building Santa Fe, NM 87501
New York	**Department of Social Services** Ten Eyck Building 40 N. Pearl Street Albany, NY 12243	**State Education Department** The University of the State of New York Albany, NY 12234
North Carolina	**Office of Child Day Care Licensing** 701 Barbour Drive Raleigh, NC 27605	**Department of Public Education** 116 W. Edenton Street Raleigh, NC 27603
North Dakota	**Department of Human Services** State Capitol Building Bismark, ND 58505	**Department of Public Instruction** State Capitol, 9th Floor Bismark, ND 58505
Ohio	**Department of Human Services** Bureau of Child Care Services 30 East Broad Street, 30th Floor Columbus, OH 43266	**Department of Education** 65 S. Front Street Columbus, OH 43266
Oklahoma	**Department of Human Services** Sequoyah Memorial Office Building P.O. Box 25352 Oklahoma City, OK 73125	**State Department of Education** 2500 North Lincoln Blvd. Oklahoma City, OK 73105
Oregon	**Children's Services Division** Day Care Unit 378–3178 198 Commercial, SE Salem, OR 97310	**Department of Education** 700 Pringle Pkwy., S.E. Salem, OR 97310
Pennsylvania	**Department of Public Welfare** Office of Children, Youth, & Families Bureau of Child Day-Care Services P.O. Box 2675 Harrisburg, PA 17105	**Department of Education** 333 Market Street P.O. Box 911 Harrisburg, PA 17126

Rhode Island	**Department of Children and Their Families** Day Care Licensing Unit 610 Mount Pleasant Ave. Providence, RI 02908	**Department of Education** 22 Hayes Street Providence, RI 02908
South Carolina	**Department of Social Services** Children and Family Services P.O. Box 1520 Columbia, SC 29202	**State Department of Education** Rutledge Office Building Columbia, SC 29201
South Dakota	**Department of Social Services** Richard F. Kneip Building 700 Governors Drive Pierre, SD 57501	**Department of Education and Cultural Affairs** Richard F. Kneip Building 700 Governors Drive Pierre, SD 57501
Tennessee	**Department of Human Services** 400 Deaderick Street Nashville, TN 37219	**Department of Education** 125 Cordell Hall Building Nashville, TN 37219
Texas	**Department of Human Resources** Licensing Division P.O. Box 149030 MC 550–W Austin, TX 78714	**Texas Education Agency** W. B. Travis Building 1701 N. Congress Austin, TX 78701
Utah	**Department of Social Services** Division of Family Services 120 North, 200 West Room 324 Salt Lake City, UT 84103	**State Board of Education** 250 E. 5th South Salt Lake City, UT 84111
Vermont	**Department of Social and Rehabilitative Services** Division of Licensing and Regulation 103 South Main Street Waterbury, VT 05676	**Department of Education** State Office Building Montpelier, VT 05602
Virginia	**Department of Social Services** Blair Building 8007 Discovery Drive Richmond, VA 23229	**Department of Education** P.O. Box 60 Richmond, VA 23216
Washington	**Department of Social and Health Services** 500 Capital Blvd. Olympia, WA 98504	**Department of Public Instruction** 600 South Washington Olympia, WA 98504
West Virginia	**Department of Human Resources** 1900 Washington Street, East Charleston, WV 25305	**Dept of Education** Building 6, Room B-304 Capitol Complex Charleston, WV 25305
Wisconsin	**Department of Health and Social Services** Division of Community Services 1 West Wilson Street P.O. Box 7851 Madison, WI 53707	**Department of Public Instruction** 125 South Webster Street P.O. Box 7841 Madison, WI 53707

Wyoming	**Department of Health and Social Services** Hathaway Building Cheyenne, WY 82002	**State Department of Education** Hathaway Building Cheyenne, WY 82002
American Somoa	**Department of Health** Fagaalu Pago Pago, AS 96799	**Department of Education** Utulei Pago Pago, AS 96799
Guam	**Department of Public Health and Social Services** P.O. Box 2816 Agana, GU 96910	**Department of Education** P.O. Box DE Agana, GU 96910
N. Mariana Islands	**Department of Education** Saipan, CM 96950	
Puerto Rico	**Department of Social Services** P.O. Box 11398, Fernandez Juncos Station Santuree, PR 00910	**Department of Education** P.O. Box 759 Hato Rey, PR 00919
Virgin Islands	**Youth Services Commission** Hamilton House St. Croix, VI 00820	**Department of Education** P.O. Box I, Christiansted St. Croix, VI 00820

B

EARLY CHILDHOOD PROFESSIONAL ORGANIZATIONS AND INFORMATION SOURCES

(Reproduced with permission. Sciarra, D. J., and Dorsey, A. G. (1990). Developing and administering a child care center. 2d ed. Albany, NY: Delmar Publishers, Inc.)

Administration for Children, Youth and Families (ACYF)
Department of Health and Human Services
P.O. Box 1182
Washington, DC 20013

Administration for Children, Youth and Families (ACYF)
Head Start Division
P.O. Box 1182
Washington, DC 20013

American Academy of Pediatrics
P.O. Box 927 141 Northwest Point Blvd.
Elk Grove Village, IL 60007
(800) 433–9016

American Association of Elementary-Kindergarten-Nursery Education(EKNE)
NEA Center
1202 16th St. N.W.
Washington, DC 20036

American Association for Gifted Children
15 Gramercy Park
New York, NY 10003

American Association of School Administrators
1801 N. Moore Street
Arlington, VA 22209–9988
(703) 528–0700

American Council of Education (ACE)
785 Massachusetts Avenue, N.W.
Washington, DC 20036

American Educational Research Association (AERA)
1230 17th St. N.W.
Washington, DC 20036

American Federation of Teachers (AFT)
11 DuPont Circle, N.W.
Washington, DC 20036

American Home Economics Association
2010 Massachusetts Ave. N.W.
Washington, DC 20036

American Library Association
Children's Services Division
50 East Huron Street
Chicago, IL 60611

American Management Association
135 W. 50th St.
New York, NY 10020
(202) 586–8100

American Montessori Society (AMS)
150 Fifth Ave., Suite #203
New York, NY 10011
(212) 924–3209

American Medical Association
535 N. Dearborn Street
Chicago, IL 60610

American Speech, Language and Hearing Association
10801 Rockville Pike
Rockville, MD 20852
(800) 638–8255

Appalachian Regional Commission
1666 Connecticut Avenue, N.W.
Washington, DC 20235
(212) 673–7893

Association for the Care of Children's Health
3615 Wisconsin Avenue, N.W.
Washington, DC 20016
(202) 244–1801

Association for Childhood Education International (ACEI)
11141 Georgia Ave., Suite 200
Wheaton, MD 20902
(301) 942–2443

Association Montessori Internationale
170 West Scholfield Road
Rochester, NY 14617–4599
(716) 544–6709

Association Montessori Internationale
Koninginneweg 161
1075 CN Amsterdam
Holland Phone: (020) 79–89–32

Association for Supervision and Curriculum Development (ASCD)
1250 North Pitt Street
Alexandria, VA 22314–2798

Black Child Developmental Institute, Inc. (BCDI)
1028 Connecticut Avenue, N.W.
Suite 514
Washington, DC 20036

California Child Care Resource and Referral Network
320 Judah St., Suite 2
San Francisco, CA 94122

Center for Disease Control
Atlanta, GA 30333
(404) 329–3091

Center for Parenting Studies
Wheelock College
200 The Riverway
Boston, MA 02215–4176
(617) 734–5200

Center for Urban Education
33 West 42nd Street
New York, NY 10036

Chicago Commons Association
Milesquare Community Center
124 North Hoyne Ave. #105
Chicago, IL 60612
(312) 421–4223

Child Care Law Center
22 Second Street, 5th Floor
San Francisco, CA 94105
(415) 495–5498

Child Development Service Bureau
400 Sixth St., S.W.
Washington, DC 20201

Child Study Association of America
9 East 89th Street
New York, NY 10003

Child Welfare League of America
440 First St. N.W. Suite 400
Washington, DC 20001
(202) 638–2952

Children's Defense Fund
122 C Street, N.W.
Washington, DC 20001
(202) 628–8787

Council for Early Childhood Professional Recognition
1718 Connecticut Ave. N.W.
Washington, DC 20009
(800) 424–4310 or (202) 265–9090

Council for Exceptional Children (CEC)
Division of Early Childhood (DEC)
1920 Association Drive
Reston, VA 22091–1589
(703) 620–3660

Council on Interracial Books for Children
1841 Broadway, Suite 500
New York, NY 10023
(212) 757–5339

Directors' Network
Exchange Press, Inc.
PO Box 2890
Redmond, WA 98073–2890
(206) 883–9394

Ecumenical Child Care Network
National Council of Churches
475 Riverside Drive, Rm 572
New York, NY 10115–0050

Education Development Center (EDC)
55 Chapel Street
Newton, MA 02160

ERIC Clearinghouse on Elementary and Early
Childhood Education (ERIC/EECE)
University of Illinois, College of Education
805 West Pennsylvania Ave.
Urbana, IL 61801–4897
(217) 333–1386

ERIC Clearinghouse on Handicapped and Gifted
Children Council for Exceptional Children
1920 Association Drive
Reston, VA 22091
(703) 620–3660

Gesell Institute for Human Development
310 Prospect Place
New Haven, CT 06511
(203) 485–2000 or (800) 624–4281

Government Information Services
Education Funding Research Council
1611 N. Kent Street, Suite 508
Arlington, VA 22209
(703) 528–1082

Head Start Association, Inc.
280 N. St. Clair St.
Painesville, OH 44077
(216) 352–8981

High/Scope Educational Research Foundation
600 N. River Street
Ypsilanti, MI 48198–2898
(313) 485–2000

Institute for Childhood Resources
1005 Market Street, Rm 207
San Francisco, CA 94103

International Child Resource Institute
1810 Hopkins Street
Berkeley, CA 94707
(415) 525–8866

International Reading Association
800 Barksdale Rd., P.O. Box 8139
Newark, DE 19714

Jewish Publication Society of America
60 E. 42nd St.
New York, NY 10165

League Against Child Abuse
1 East State St.
Columbus, OH 43215

Military Early Childhood Alliance (MECA)
934 Avenida del Sol, N.E.
Albuquerque, NM 87110

National Association for Child Care Management
(NACCM)
104 Sweetwater Hills Drive
Longwood, FL 32779
(305) 862–7825

National Association of Child Care Professionals
P.O. Box 256
Palatine, IL 60078–0256

National Association for the Education of Young
Children (NAEYC)
1834 Connecticut Ave. N.W.
Washington, DC 20009–5786
(202) 232–8777 or (800) 424–2460

National Association of Elementary School
Principals
1615 Duke Street
Alexandria, VA 22314–3483
(703) 684–3345

National Association for Family Day Care (NAFDC)
815 Fifteenth St. N.W., Suite 928
Washington, DC 20005–2201
(202) 387–1281

National Association of Hospital Affiliated Child
Care Programs
Hannah Sampson, Documensions
11 N. Batavia Avenue #2B
Batavia, IL 60510

National Association of State Boards of Education
1012 Cameron Street
Alexandria, VA 22314
(703) 684–4000

National Black Child Development Institute (NBCDI)
1463 Rhode Island Ave. N.W.
Washington, DC 20005–5493
(202) 387–1281

National Center for Clinical Infant Programs
733 Fifteenth St. N.W., Suite 912
Washington, DC 20005–2112
(202) 347–0308

National Child Care Association (NCCA)
920 Green Street
Conyers, GA 30207
(800) 543–7161

National Child Labor Committee
1501 Broadway, Room 1111
New York, NY 10036

National Coalition for Campus Child Care, Inc.
UMW, P.O. Box 413
Milwaukee, WI 53201
(414) 229-5384

National Council of Jewish Women (NCJW)
Center for the Child
53 West 23rd Street
New York, NY 10010

National Dairy Council
6300 North River Road
Rosemont, IL 60018-4233
(312) 696-1020

National Education Association (NEA)
1201 16th St., N.W.
Washington, DC 20036

National Education Task Force
De La Raza
College of New Mexico
Albuquerque, NM 87106

National Head Start Association
1309 King Street, Suite 200
Alexandria, VA 22314-2928
(703) 739-0875 FAX: (703) 739-0878

National Indian Education Advisory Council
College of Education
University of New Mexico, Office of the Dean
Albuquerque, NM 87131

(Non)Sexist Child Development Project
Women's Action Alliance, Inc.
370 Lexington Ave., Rm. 603
New York, NY 10017

North American Montessori Teachers Association (NAMTA)
2859 Scarborough Rd.
Cleveland, Heights, OH 44118
(216)371-1566

Parent Cooperative Preschools International, U.S. Office
P.O. Box 90410
Indianapolis, IN 46290
(317) 849-0992

Puerto Rican Association for Community Affairs, Inc.
411 East 10th Street
New York, NY 10009

Save the Children
1340 Spring Street, N.W.
Atlanta, GA 30309
(404) 885-1578

School-Age Child Care Project
Wellesley College
Center for Research on Women
Wellesley, MA 02181
(617) 235-0320 or (617) 431-1453

Society for Research in Child Development (SRCD) at the University of Chicago Press
5720 South Woodlawn Avenue
Chicago, IL 60637
(312) 702-7470

Southern Association on Children Under Six (SACUS)
P.O. Box 5403 Brady Station
Little Rock, AR 72215
(501) 663-0353

SUMMA Associates, Inc.
Child Care Benefits Planning
56 E. Holly Street, Suite 215
Pasadena, CA 91103
(818) 796-8258

Superintendent of Documents
Government Printing Office
Washington, DC 20402-9325
(202) 783-3238

The Children's Book Council, Inc.
67 Irving Place
New York, NY 10003
(212) 254-2666

The Feminist Press at The City University of New York
311 E. 94th Street
New York, NY 10128
(212) 360-5790

U.S. Consumer Product Safety Commission
Washington, DC 20207
Att. Office of Information and Public Affairs
(800) 638-2772

U.S. National Committee of OMEP
World Organization for Early Childhood Education
1718 Connecticut Avenue, N.W., Suite 500
Washington, DC 20009

U.S. Department of Health and Human Services
Administration for Children, Youth and Families
(ACYF)
Washington, DC 20201

U.S. Office of Education
400 Maryland Avenue, S.W.
Washington, DC 20202

Women's Action Alliance, Inc.
370 Lexington Avenue
New York, NY 10017

Work/Family Directions, Inc.
Nine Galen Street, Suite 230
Watertown, MA 02172
(617) 923–1535
(800) 346–1535

Work and Family Life Studies/Research Division
Bank Street College
610 West 112th Street
New York, NY 10025
(212) 663–7200

C

THE NATIONAL ASSOCIATION FOR THE EDUCATION OF YOUNG CHILDREN'S CODE OF ETHICAL CONDUCT

(Reproduced with permission. The National Association for the Education of Young Children. 1989. Code of ethical conduct. Young Children, 45(1): 25–20.)

Preamble

NAEYC recognizes that many daily decisions required of those who work with young children are of a moral and ethical nature. The NAEYC Code of Ethical Conduct offers guidelines for responsible behavior and sets forth a common basis for resolving the principal ethical dilemmas encountered in early childhood education. The primary focus is on daily practice with children and their families in programs for children from birth to 8 years of age: preschools, child care centers, family day care homes, kindergartens, and primary classrooms. Many of the provisions also apply to specialists who do not work directly with children, including program administrators, parent educators, college professors, and child care licensing specialists.

Standards of ethical behavior in early childhood education are based on commitment to core values that are deeply rooted in the history of our field. We have committed ourselves to:

Appreciating childhood as a unique and valuable stage of the human life cycle

Basing our work with children on knowledge of child development

Appreciating and supporting the close ties between the child and family

Recognizing that children are best understood in the context of family, culture, and society

Respecting the dignity, worth, and uniqueness of each individual (child, family member, and colleague)

Helping children and adults achieve their full potential in the context of relationships that are based on trust, respect, and positive regard

The Code sets forth a conception of our professional responsibilities in four sections, each addressing an arena of professional relationships: 1) children, 2) families, 3) colleagues, and 4) community and society. Each section includes an introduction to the primary responsibilities of the early childhood practitioner in that arena, a set of principles defining practices that are required, prohibited, and permitted.

The ideals reflect the aspirations of practitioners. The principles are intended to guide conduct and assist practitioners in resolving ethical dilemmas encountered in the field. There is not necessarily a corresponding principle for each ideal. Both ideals and principles are intended to direct practitioners to those questions which, when responsibly answered, will provide the basis for conscientious decision making. While the Code provides specific direction for addressing some ethical dilemmas, many others will require the practitioner to combine the guidance of the Code with sound professional judgment.

The ideals and principles in this Code present a shared conception of professional responsibility that affirms our commitment to the core values of our field. The Code publicly acknowledges the responsibilities that we in the field have assumed and in so doing supports ethical behavior in our work. Practitioners who face ethical dilemmas are urged to seek guidance in the applicable parts of the Code and in the spirit that informs the whole.

Section I: Ethical Responsibilities to Children

Childhood is a unique and valuable stage in the life cycle. Our paramount responsibility is to provide safe, healthy, nurturing, and responsive settings for children. We are committed to supporting children's development by cherishing individual differences, by helping them learn to live and work cooperatively, and by promoting their self-esteem.

Ideals

I-1.1 To be familiar with the knowledge base of early childhood education and to keep current through continuing education and in-service training.

I-1.2 To base program practices upon current knowledge in the field of child development and related disciplines and upon particular knowledge of each child.

I-1.3 To recognize and respect the uniqueness and the potential of each child.

I-1.4 To appreciate the special vulnerability of children.

I-1.5 To create and maintain safe and healthy settings that foster children's social, emotional, intellectual, and physical development and that respect their dignity and their contributions.

I-1.6 To support the right of children with special needs to participate, consistent with their ability, in regular early childhood programs.

Principles

P-1.1 Above all, we shall not harm children. We shall not participate in practices that are disrespectful, degrading, dangerous, exploitative, intimidating, psychologically damaging, or physically harmful to children. **This principle has precedence over all others in the Code.**

P-1.2 We shall not participate in practices that discriminate against children by denying benefits, giving special advantages, or excluding them from programs or activities on the basis of their race, religion, sex, national origin, or the status, behavior or beliefs of their parents. (This principle does not apply to programs that have a lawful mandate to provide services to a particular population of children.)

P-1.3 We shall involve all of those with relevant knowledge (including staff and parents) in decisions concerning a child.

P-1.4 When, after appropriate efforts have been made with a child and the family, the child still does not appear to be benefitting from a program, we shall communicate our concern to the family in a positive way and offer them assistance in finding a more suitable setting.

P-1.5 We shall be familiar with the symptoms of child abuse and neglect and know community procedures for addressing them.

P-1.6 When we have evidence of child abuse or neglect, we shall report the evidence to the appropriate community agency and follow up to ensure that appropriate action has been taken. When possible, parents will be informed that the referral has been made.

P-1.7 When another person tells us of their suspicion that a child is being abused or neglected but we lack evidence, we shall assist that person in taking appropriate action to protect the child.

P-1.8 When a child protective agency fails to provide adequate protection for abused or neglected children, we acknowledge a collective ethical responsibility to work toward improvement of these services.

Section II: Ethical Responsibilities to Families

Families are of primary importance in children's development. (The term **family** may include others, besides parents, who are responsibly involved with the child.) Because the family and the early childhood educator have a common interest in the child's welfare, we acknowledge a primary responsibility to bring about collaboration between the home and school in ways that enhance the child's development.

Ideals:

I-2.1 To develop relationships of mutual trust with the families we serve.

I-2.2 To acknowledge and build upon strengths and competencies as we support families in the task of nurturing children.

I-2.3 To respect the dignity of each family and its culture, customs, and beliefs.

I-2.4 To respect families' childrearing values and their rights to make decisions for their children.

I-2.5 To interpret each child's progress to parents within the framework of a developmental perspective and to help families understand and appreciate the value of developmentally appropriate early childhood programs.

I-2.6 To help family members improve their understanding of their children and to enhance their skills as parents.

I-2.7 To participate in building support networks for families by providing them with opportunities to interact with program staff and families.

Principles

P-2.1 We shall not deny family members access to their child's classroom or program setting.

P-2.2 We shall inform families of program philosophy, policies, and personnel qualifications, and explain why we teach as we do.

P-2.3 We shall inform families of and, when appropriate, involve them in policy decisions.

P-2.4 We shall inform families of and, when appropriate, involve them in significant decisions affecting their child.

P-2.5 We shall inform the family of accidents involving their child, of risks such as exposures to contagious disease that may result in infection, and of events that might result in psychological damage.

P-2.6 We shall not permit or participate in research that could in any way hinder the education or development of the children in our programs. Families shall be fully informed of any

P-2.7   We shall not engage in or support exploitation of families. We shall not use our relationship with a family for private advantage or personal gain, or enter into relationships with family members that might impair our effectiveness in working with children.

P-2.8   We shall develop written policies for the protection of confidentiality and the disclosure of children's records. The policy documents shall be made available to all program personnel, and families. Disclosure of children's records beyond family members, program personnel, and consultants having an obligation of confidentiality shall require familial consent (except in cases of abuse or neglect).

P-2.9   We shall maintain confidentiality and shall respect the family's right to privacy, refraining from disclosure of confidential information and intrusion into family life. However, when we are concerned about a child's welfare, it is permissible to reveal confidential information to agencies and individuals who may be able to act in the child's interest.

P-2.10   In cases where family members are in conflict we shall work openly, sharing our observations of the child, to help all parties involved make informed decisions. We shall refrain from becoming an advocate for one party.

P-2.11   We shall be familiar with and appropriately use community resources and professional services that support families. After a referral has been made, we shall follow up to ensure that services have been adequately provided.

Section III: Ethical Responsibilities to Colleagues

In a caring, cooperative work place human dignity is respected, professional satisfaction is promoted, and positive relationships are modeled. Our primary responsibility in this arena is to establish and maintain settings and relationships that support productive work and meet professional needs.

A—Responsibilities to Co-Workers

Ideals

I-3A.1   To establish and maintain relationships of trust and cooperation with co-workers.

I-3A.2   To share resources and information with co-workers.

I-3A.3   To support co-workers in meeting their professional needs and in their professional development.

I-3A.4   To accord co-workers due recognition of professional achievement.

Principles

P-3A.1   When we have concern about the professional behavior of a co-worker, we shall first let that person know of our concern and attempt to resolve the matter collegially.

P-3A.2   We shall exercise care in expressing views regarding the personal attributes or professional conduct of co-workers. Statements should be based on firsthand knowledge and relevant to the interests of children and programs.

B—Responsibilities to Employers

Ideals

I-3B.1   To assist the program in providing the highest quality of service.

I-3B.2   To maintain loyalty to the program and uphold its reputation.

Principles

P-3B.1   When we do not agree with program policies, we shall first attempt to effect change through constructive action within the organization.

P-3B.2   We shall speak or act on behalf of an organization only when authorized. We shall take care to note when we are speaking for the organization and when we are expressing a personal judgment.

C—Responsibilities to Employees

Ideals

I-3C.1   To promote policies and working conditions that foster competence, well-being, and self-esteem in staff members.

I-3C.2   To create a climate of trust and candor that will enable staff to speak and act in the best interests of children, families, and the field of early childhood education.

I-3C.3   To strive to secure an adequate livelihood for those who work with or on behalf of young children.

Principles

P-3C.1   In decisions concerning children and programs, we shall appropriately utilize the training, experience, and expertise of staff members.

P-3C.2   We shall provide staff members with working conditions that permit them to carry out their responsibilities, timely and nonthreatening evaluation procedures, written grievance procedures, constructive feedback, and opportunities for continuing professional development and advancement.

P-3C.3   We shall develop and maintain comprehensive written personnel policies that define program standards and, when applicable, that specify the extent to which employees are accountable for their conduct outside the work place. These policies shall be given to new staff members and shall be available for review by all staff members.

P-3C.4   Employees who do not meet program standards shall be informed of areas of concern and, when possible, assisted in improving their performance.

P-3C.5   Employees who are dismissed shall be informed of the reasons for their termination. When a dismissal is for cause, justification must be based on evidence of inadequate or inappropriate behavior that is accurately documented, current, and available for the employee to review.

P-3C.6   In making evaluations and recommendations, judgments shall be based on fact and relevant to the interests of children and programs.

P-3C.7   Hiring and promotion shall be based solely on a person's record of accomplishment and ability to carry out the responsibilities of the position.

P3C.8   In hiring, promotion, and provision of training, we shall not participate in any form of discrimination based on race, religion, sex, national origin, handicap, age, or sexual preference. We shall be familiar with laws and regulations that pertain to employment discrimination.

Section IV: Ethical Responsibilities to Community and Society

Early childhood programs operate within a context of an immediate community made up of families and other institutions concerned with children's welfare. Our responsibilities to the community are to provide programs that meet its needs and to cooperate with agencies and professions that share responsibilities for children. Because the larger society has a measure of responsibility for the welfare and protection of children, and because of our specialized expertise in child development, we acknowledge an obligation to serve as a voice for children everywhere.

Ideals

I-4.1 To provide the community with high-quality, culturally sensitive programs and service.

I-4.2 To promote cooperation among agencies and professions concerned with the welfare of young children, their families, and their teachers.

I-4.3 To work, through education, research, and advocacy, toward an environmentally safe world in which children are adequately fed, sheltered, and nurtured.

I-4.4 To work, through education, research, and advocacy, toward a society in which all young children have access to quality programs.

I-4.5 To promote knowledge and understanding of young children and their needs. To work toward greater social acknowledgement of children's rights and greater social acceptance of responsibility for their well-being.

I-4.6 To support policies and laws that promote the well-being of children and families. To oppose those that impair their well-being. To cooperate with other individuals and groups in these efforts.

I-4.7 To further the professional development of the field of early childhood education and to strengthen its commitment to realizing its core values as reflected in this Code.

Principles

P-4.1 We shall communicate openly and truthfully about the nature and extent of services that we provide.

P-4.2 We shall not accept or continue to work in positions for which we are personally unsuited or professionally unqualified. We shall not offer services that we do not have the competence, qualifications, or resources to provide.

P-4.3 We shall be objective and accurate in reporting the knowledge upon which we base our program practices.

P-4.4 We shall cooperate with other professionals who work with children and their families.

P-4.5 We shall not hire or recommend for employment any person who is unsuited for a position with respect to competence, qualifications, or character.

P-4.6 We shall report the unethical or incompetent behavior of a colleague to a supervisor when information resolution is not effective.

P-4.7 We shall be familiar with laws and regulations that serve to protect the children in our programs.

P-4.8 We shall not participate in practices which are in violation of laws and regulations that protect the children in our programs.

P-4.9 When we have evidence that an early childhood program is violating laws or regulations protecting children, we shall report it to persons responsible for the program. If compliance is not accomplished within a reasonable time, we will report the violation to appropriate authorities who can be expected to remedy the situation.

P-4.10 When we have evidence that an agency or a professional charged with providing services to children, families, or teachers is failing to meet its obligations, we acknowledge a collective ethical responsibility to report the problem to appropriate authorities or to the public.

P-4.11 When a program violates or requires its employees to violate this Code, it is permissible, after fair assessment of the evidence, to disclose the identity of that program.

D

SUGGESTED MATERIALS LIST

(from State of Nevada Regulations and Standards for Child Care Facilities, Department of Human Resources, 1989)

Art

Paper: butcher, construction, newsprint, colored tissue, cardboard & paper plates
Paint: finger, tempera, & watercolors—with various brushes, easels, drying rack, aprons
Glue & paste
Tape & holder
Scissors & holder
Magazines and wallpaper books
Clay: playdough, wet clay, modeling clay, rolling pins & clay hammers
Weaving materials
Collage items: cloth scraps, ribbons, yarn, sequins, glitter, straws, beads & buttons, styrofoam packing
Writing materials: pens, pencils, crayons & felt pens, containers
Chalk board & chalk

Block Play

Unit blocks, lumber scraps, cardboard building blocks, boxes, small cars, trucks, trains, planes, people & animals
Pictures: cut from magazines of roads, bridges, airports, construction equipment, fire engines, farms & cities
Push & pull toys

Dramatic Play/Housekeeping

Child sized furniture: kitchen, bedroom & living room, labeled drawers, containers, mirrors, dolls & doll clothes, stuffed animals
Doll furniture: high chairs, bassinets, beds, carriages, blankets & pillows
Dress-up clothes, costumes
Telephones
Kitchen items: dishes, pots, pans, measuring cups, silverware, bowls, utensils, funnels, sieves, & empty food containers & cans
Desk supplies
Store set-up

Puppets and stage
Cleaning items: brooms, mops, warm soapy water in dishpan, sponges, aprons & dish towels, wastebasket
Dollhouse & furniture, people

Language/Library

Table & chairs, rocking chair, carpet, pillows, book rack
Records & tapes: storage, blank tapes
Film strips
Record player & tape recorder
Writing materials: paper, scissors
Picture file
Mailbox
Carefully selected books: variety of subjects, teacher-made; child-made, published, resource books, newspapers, magazines, & catalogs
Puppets & stage
Flannel board & objects, stories
Magnetic board & letters
Games: lotto games, matching pictures, letter games, puzzles, sequence cards, rhyming & language games, kinesthetic letters, alphabet packets, ABC packets, feelie box, story starter cards
Walkie talkies
Camera & film

Manipulative Activities

Table-top blocks: legos, Lincoln logs, bristle blocks
Puzzles
Large wooden beads, spools, heavy string
Nuts/bolts
Lacing materials, zippers, buttons
Peg boards, hooks, pegs

Math

Math games & activities: seriation, classification, matching number concepts, sorting, sequencing, patterning & spatial relationships, puzzles, number cards, measuring cups & spoons, rulers
Cooking supplies & activities
Water & sand play
Block play
Flannelboard: games, shapes, & numbers
Comparison songs & music
Parquetry
Dominoes
Cuisenaire rods
Clocks
Tape measures
Cash register & play money
Wooden beads
Geometric shapes
Calendars

Science

Plants: sweet potatoes, carrot tops, pumpkin seeds, lentils, corn, bird seed, terrarium

Nature collections: shells, stones, pebbles, pods, seeds, nuts, leaves
Aquarium
Insect containers
Magnets
Prisms
Scales, thermometer, compass
Pulley springs & gears
Magnifying glass
Sniff & smell bottles: cinnamon, onion, coffee, lemon, orange, nutmeg, cloves & banana
Inside pets: guinea pigs, snails, goldfish, mice, kittens, hamsters, rats, turtles, tadpoles & snakes
Outside pets: rabbits, ducks, land tortoises, chickens, lambs & goats
Incubator
Digging area: construction work shovels, wheelbarrows
Appliance crates & large boxes
Gardening area: simple garden with radishes, lettuce, corn & tomatoes, watering can, flower boxes
Conservation & ecology activities
Birdfeeder

Music

Rhythm instruments: drums, xylophones, triangles, rhythm sticks & rattles
Record player & records
Tape recorder & tapes
Autoharps, piano, & guitar
Props for dancing: scarves, crepe paper streamers, balloons
Materials for homemade instruments

Outdoor Play

Swings, slides & climbers
Playhouse
Wheeltoys: trikes, wagons & scooters
Wheeltoy area: hard smooth area, garage for parking, stop signs, traffic signs, gas station (oil drum with hose & hats)
Sand area: gardening tools, toys & containers
Balls, boxes, tires, planks

Sand/Water Area

Sand: digging tools, toy props, buckets, cans, shovels, spoons, bowls, jello molds, plastic bottles & funnels, water, containers with textured materials
Water: hose adjusted for steady trickle for child use outdoors, pans of water with dishes, cups, plastic bottles & pitchers, tubs of water for boats, floating objects, extra clothes, aprons, house paint brushes, egg beaters

Water Table

Containers: round, oval, oblong, square, large, small, graded in size, shallow, deep, transparent, opaque, metal & plastic, wooden materials
Rubber or plastic aprons
Spoons, ladles, and scoops
Teapot, watering can, sieves, tea strainer, funnels, plastic mugs with holes in side or bottom, plastic rings, plastic or wooden toys
Bubble pipes, circular colander, squeegee bottle, plastic balls with holes, corks

Woodworking

Sturdy tools: hammers, saws, vise, screwdrivers, hand drill, pliers, rulers, carpenter's pencil & scrap soft wood, nails & screws
Workbench
Tool storage, boxes for storage
Wood glue, corks to hold nails in place
Safety rules
Scrap materials: bottle caps, cloth, empty thread spools, flexible wire

Classroom

Lavatory: paper towels & holder, mirror, liquid soap, tissue
Rest: cots & cribs, blankets, sheets
Kitchen: Small glasses, plates, utensils, paper napkins, sponges, serving bowls, platters, serving spoons (Note: some states require that plates and utensils be single service/disposable)

INDEX

A

Absenteeism, 67
Abused children, 145
Accident policies, 142–43, 149–50
Accreditation, 215–16, 222
Accreditation Criteria and Procedures, 215, 222
ACEI (Association of Childhood Education International), 41
Activity plan, 126, 135–36
Advertising. *See also* Marketing
    brochures, 15, 25–26, 199
    for new staff, 41, 53
    press releases, 198, 199, 203
Advocacy, 71, 84
Aggression, 186
Alien Registration Card, 42
Allergies, food, 159, 160, 172
Anemia, 159
Application forms, 41–42, 54
Aronson, Susan, 142
Arrival-Departure Card, 42
Articles of Incorporation, 31–33, 35–37
Art supplies, 86–87, 245
Association of Childhood Education International (ACEI), 41
Audit, 94

B

Bank accounts, 94
Behavior problems
    food and, 159
    parent-teacher communication and, 186
Birthday parties, 159, 171
Block play, 88, 245
Board of directors, 29–31
    areas of expertise of, 29–30
    parents on, 30, 176, 181
    purchasing and, 90
    responsibilities of, 30–31
Bookkeeping, 93
Books, 125, 246
Brainstorming, 12, 18
Breakfast meetings, 199, 207
Breastfeeding, 158, 170
Brochures, 15, 25–26, 199
Budget, 87–89, 101–4, 107
Building
    costs of, 86–87
    leasing space vs., 113
    regulations concerning, 112–13, 118
Bylaws, 31–33, 35–37

C

Celebrations, 159, 171
Certification agencies, 225–30
Certified Public Accountant (CPA), 94
Checklist for program evaluation, 215, 219–22
Child and Adult Care Food Program, 158, 161–62
Child and Youth Care Forum, 33
Child care center
    brochure on, 15, 25–26, 199
    building, 86–87, 112–13, 118
    design of, 113–16, 117–22
    equipping, 86–87, 88, 97–100, 245–48
    for-profit vs. not-for-profit, 29, 94, 95
    location of, 112
    naming, 14, 23
    need for, 10
    parental involvement with, 175, 181–82, 195–96
    planning, 10–13, 17–22, 112–13, 117–19, 121–22
    sponsorship of, 11, 28–29
    start-up costs of, 86
Child Care Information Exchange, 33, 43, 64, 142, 198
Child care plan, 126–28, 137–39

Child care programs
    evaluation of, 213–14, 217–20
    privately run, 29
    publicly run, 28
Child care worker. *See also* Staff
    defined, 5
    salary of, 43, 66–67, 88
Childhood Education, 33
Children
    abused, 145
    custody of, 176
    with disabilities, 125, 127, 145
    ethical responsibilities to, 238–39
    missing, 143
    obese, 159
    underweight, 159
Children's Defense Fund, 43
Children's records, 128–29, 140, 176, 193
Child Welfare, 33
Civil Rights Act of 1964, 41
Classroom, furnishings and supplies for, 86–87, 88, 97–100, 114, 245–48. *See also* Physical environment
Code of Ethical Conduct of the National Association for the Education of Young Children (NAEYC), 237–43
Code of ethics, 70, 82–83, 237–43
Colleagues, ethical responsibilities to, 240–42
Communication, with parents, 176–80, 187–94, 223–24
Community
    ethical responsibilities to, 242–43
    medical and psychological resources of, 146, 153
    sources of information in, 14–15, 231–35
Competition, in cooperative learning groups, 2, 3
Complaints, 198
Compromise, 3
Computer programs, 93
Conferences, parent-teacher, 179–80, 191–92
Confidentiality, of written records, 69, 79–80, 128, 129
Conflict management, 67
Consultants, health care, 146–47
Contracts, 94
Cooking, 157
Cooperative learning groups, 2–8
    benefits of, 2
    diversity in, 5
    evaluation of, 8
    instructor's role in, 5–7
    interaction in, 3–4
    lectures in, 6, 7
    pitfalls of, 7
    scheduling of, 6
    student/group member's role in, 3–5
Cooperativeness and cooperative skills, 2, 6
Corporation, 29–38
    board of directors of, 29–31
    bylaws of, 31–33, 35–37
    defined, 29
    executive director of, 31

    legal requirements for, 93–95
Costs
    of equipment and materials, 86–87, 88, 97–100
    in operating budget, 87–89, 101–4
    salaries, 43, 66–67, 88
    start-up, 86
Co-workers, ethical responsibilities to, 240
CPR training, 64, 142, 143
Cultural diversity, 175–76, 185
Curriculum
    health and safety in, 146–47, 154
    for infants and toddlers, 125, 126
    planning, 124–28, 131–36
Custody rights, 176

D

Day Care and Early Education, 33
Decision making, 10–12, 18
Design, 113–16, 117–22
Developmentally appropriate practice in early childhood programs serving children from birth through age 8, 125
Differential staffing, 40
Director. *See also* Board of directors
    bookkeeping and, 93
    in curriculum planning, 124, 129, 131–33
    executive, 31
    finances and, 90, 109
    hiring of, 33
    legal matters and, 109
    mealtimes and, 157
    parents and, 174, 186
    role of, 33, 38
    staff evaluation by, 65
    staff management and, 62
    in staff meetings, 62–63
    staff supervision by, 66–67
    staff training and, 63–64
Disabilities, children with, 125, 127, 145
Disease. *See* Illness
Divorce, 145, 176
Dramatic play, materials list for, 245–46

E

Early Childhood Environment Rating Scale, 115, 213
Emergency and accident policies, 142–43, 149–50
Employees. *See* Staff
Employer identification number, 93
Employers, ethical responsibilities to, 241
Enrollment process, 178–79
Environment. *See* Physical environment
Equipment, 86–87, 88, 97–100, 245–48
Ethics, code of, 70, 82–83, 237–43
Evaluation, 211–24
    for accreditation, 215–16, 222
    of brochures, 25
    checklist for, 215, 219–22
    of cooperative learning groups, 8

finding focus for, 212
formative, 212
group, 213
for licensing requirements, 214
parent questionnaire, 216, 223–24
process of, 212
of program, 213–14, 217–20
self-evaluation, 65, 77
of staff, 65, 77
of student performance, 4, 8
summative, 212
Executive director, 31

F

Facilitator, role in cooperative learning groups, 5–7
Families, ethical responsibilities to, 239–40. *See also* Parents
Family crises, 145
Family day care, 12
Family worker, 182
Feedback, 198
FICA (social security) reports and payments, 93, 94
Finances, 87–93
bookkeeping, 93
fund drives, 91
grant proposals, 91–93, 105–6
income, 89, 91, 103, 107
operating budget, 87–89, 101–4, 107
purchasing, 90–91, 97–100
start-up costs, 86
Fire drills, 143
Firing, 47, 66
First aid
teaching children, 146
training staff in, 64, 142, 143, 145
Floor plan, 115, 119
Food
allergies, 159, 160, 172
planning food program, 156–58, 161–69
preferences in, 157, 159, 172
resource management, 156–57
special problems with, 159–60, 170–72
Formative evaluation, 212
For-profit centers, 29, 95
Franchises, 29
Fund drives, 91
Furnishings, 86, 114

G

General partnership, 29
Goals
program evaluation and, 213, 217–18
statement of, 12, 19
Government agencies, 28
Grant proposals, 91–93, 105–6
Greenman, J., 113
Group, heterogeneous, 5. *See also* Cooperative learning groups

Group evaluation, 213

H

Handbook, for parents, 178, 187–90
Hawaii, training requirements of, 63
Head Start, 28
Health and safety, 141–54
consultants and, 146–47
in curriculum, 146–47, 154
emergency and accident policies, 142–43, 149–50
health policies, 144–45, 151–52
plan for, 142
signs of illness, 142, 147
of staff, 145
Health policies, 144–45, 151–52
Healthy Young Children: A Manual for Programs, 142
Hiring, 40–43, 47–56
application form, 41–42, 54
checking references, 42, 55
interviewing, 42–43, 56
job descriptions, 40–41, 49–52
recruiting, 41, 53
screening applicants, 42
from within, 48
Holiday parties, 159, 171
Home visits, 181
Housekeeping, materials list for, 245–46

I

Illness
procedures with, 144–45
signs of, 142, 147
of staff, 145
Immunizations, 144, 146
Income, 89, 91, 103, 107
Income tax. *See* Tax returns
Incorporation, Articles of, 31–33, 35–37
Indemnification Resolution, 94
Infant caregiving: A design for training, 158
Infants
curriculum planning for, 125, 126
information for parents of, 176, 180
nutrition for, 158, 170
physical environment of, 115
Infant/Toddler Environment Rating Scale, 114, 213
Information
for parents, 176–78, 180, 187–90, 193
sources of, 14–15, 231–35
Informational brochure, 15, 25–26, 199
Instructor, role in cooperative learning group, 5–7
Insurance, 94, 95, 108
Intake process, 178–79
Internal Revenue Service, 31
Interpersonal skills, 2, 3
Interviewing
of job applicants, 42–43, 56
of parents, 178–79
Iron deficiency, 159

J

Job applicants
  application forms for, 41–42, 54
  checking references of, 42, 55
  interviewing, 42–43, 56
  recruiting, 41, 53
  screening, 42
Job application forms, 41–42, 54
Job descriptions, 40–41, 49–52, 94
Johnson, David W., 2
Johnson, Roger T., 2

L

Language barriers, 176
Leasing space, vs. building, 113
Lectures, 6, 7
Legal requirements
  for building, 112–13, 118
  for operating child care center, 93–95
Liability, 29
Library materials, 125, 246
Licensing agencies, 225–30
Licensing requirements, 214
Licensing Requirements for Child Care Centers, 126–28
Limited partnership, 29
Local building regulations, 112–13, 118
Location of center, 112
Log, daily, 63
Logo, 199

M

Management, 62–67, 73–77
Marketing, 197–209
  breakfast meetings, 199, 207
  informational brochures, 15, 25–26, 199
  Open House, 199, 200, 205–6
  by phone, 199, 204
  press releases, 198, 199, 203
Market research, 14–15, 24
Materials and supplies, 86–87, 88, 97–100, 245–48
Math games and activities, materials list for, 246
Meal planning, 156, 157, 163–68
Mealtimes, 157–58, 169
Medical conditions, 145. *See also* Health and safety; Illness
Medical services, community, 146, 153
Medicines, 145
Meetings
  breakfast, 199, 207
  of cooperative learning groups, 6
  of parents, 180, 194
  of staff, 62–63, 73
Mentoring, 64
Menu planning, 156, 157, 163–68
Metabolism disorders, 159
Minnesota
  on child care plans, 126–28
  on communicating with parents, 177–78
  materials lists of, 86
  training requirements of, 63–64
Minnesota Association for the Education of Young Children, 198
Missing children, 143
Music, materials list for, 247

N

NAEYC. *See* National Association for the Education of Young Children
Name of center, 14, 23
National Academy of Early Childhood Programs, 215
National Association for the Education of Young Children (NAEYC), 41, 43, 44, 70
  Code of Ethical Conduct, 237–43
  on licensing and accreditation, 214, 215
  publications of, 125, 142, 215, 222
National Commission on Working Women, 10
National Day Care Study, 89
Needs assessment, 14–15, 24
Neugebauer, Roger, 198, 199
Nevada, materials list of, 245–48
News releases, 198, 199, 203
Not-for-profit centers, 29, 94
Nurse, 40, 146
Nutrition, 155–72
  breastfeeding, 158, 170
  Child and Adult Care Food Program, 158, 161–62
  food resource management, 156–57
  mealtimes, 157–58, 169
  menu planning, 156, 157, 163–68
  special food problems, 159–60, 170–72
  teaching children about, 157

O

Obesity, 159
Oklahoma, on communicating with parents, 177
Open House, 199, 200, 205–6
Operating budget, 87–89, 101–4, 107
Organizations
  professional, 70, 81, 231–35
  as sources of information, 14–15, 231–35
Orientation
  of new board members, 30–31
  of new staff members, 44, 58
Outdoor play, materials list for, 247

P

Parents, 173–96
  as board members, 30, 176, 181
  communicating with, 176–80, 187–94, 223–24
  conferences with teachers, 179–80, 191–92
  cultural diversity of, 175–76, 185
  director and, 174, 186
  divorced, 145, 176
  ethical responsibilities to, 239–40

handbook for, 178, 187–90
information for, 176–78, 180, 187–90, 193
involvement in center, 175, 181–82, 195–96
meetings of, 180, 194
preenrollment interview with, 178–79
questionnaire for, 216, 223–24
responding to concerns and feelings of, 175
single, 176
social/family worker and, 182
as volunteers, 181
Parent-teacher conferences, 179–80, 191–92
Parties, 159, 171
Partnership, 29
Peer pressure, 2
Performance criteria, 65
Personnel policies, 67–69, 78, 94
Personnel records, 67–69, 78–80
Pets, 145
Phenylketonuria (PKU), 159
Philosophy, statement of, 12, 13, 21–22
Physical disabilities, 125, 127, 145
Physical environment, 111–22
    effects of, 113–16, 120–22
    furnishing and equipping, 86–87, 88, 97–100, 114, 245–48
    planning, 112–13, 117–19, 121–22
PKU, 159
Planning
    activity/lesson plan, 126, 135–36
    chart for, 10, 17
    child care center, 10–13, 17–22, 112–13, 117–19, 121–22
    child care plan, 126–28, 137–39
    curriculum, 124–28, 131–36
    food program, 156–58, 161–69
    health and safety, 142
    physical environment, 112–13, 117–19, 121–22
    statements of purposes, goals, and philosophy in, 12–13, 19–22
Playground safety, 143
Play materials, 88, 245–46, 247
Policies
    emergency and accident policies, 142–43, 149–50
    health, 144–45, 151–52
    personnel, 67–69, 78, 94
Preenrollment interview, 178–79
Pre-K Today, 33
Prescott, Elizabeth, 113
Press releases, 198, 199, 203
Professional development, 70–71, 81–84
Professional organizations, 70, 81, 231–35
Program evaluation, 213–14, 217–20
Proprietorship, 29
Psychologist, 146, 153
Public agencies, 28
Publicity and public relations. *See* Marketing
Purchasing, 90–91, 97–100
Purposes, statement of, 12, 20

Q

Questionnaire for parents, 216, 223–24

R

Recognition, 67
Records
    children's, 128–29, 140, 176, 193
    personnel, 67–69, 78–80
Recruiting, 41, 53
References, checking, 42, 55
Research, market, 14–15, 24
Rhode Island, staffing requirements of, 40

S

Safety. *See* Health and safety
Salaries, 43, 66–67, 88
Sand area, materials list for, 247
Sanitation procedures, 144
Schedules
    of cooperative learning groups, 6
    in curriculum planning, 124, 126, 134
    for preschoolers, 134
    for staff, 44, 57
    of staff meetings, 62
School Lunch Program, 156
Science activities, materials list for, 246–47
SCORE (Service Corporation of Retired Executives), 93
Screening job applicants, 42
Script, telephone, 199, 204
Self-esteem, 145
Self-evaluation, 65, 77
Service Corporation of Retired Executives (SCORE), 93
Sick leave, 145
Sickness. *See* Illness
Simulation, 3
Single parents, 176
Small Business Institute, 93
Social Security Act, 156
Social security (FICA) reports and payments, 93, 94
Social skills, 2, 3
Social worker, 40, 182
Society, ethical responsibilities to, 242–43
Sole proprietorship, 29
Space, leasing, 113. *See also* Physical environment
Sponsorship, 11, 28–29
Staff, 39–84
    coordinating duties of, 44–45, 57
    differential staffing, 40
    ethical responsibilities to, 241–42
    evaluating, 65, 77
    health and safety of, 145
    health care consultants, 146
    hiring, 40–43, 47–56
    management of, 62–67, 73–77
    mealtime guidelines for, 157–58, 169

meetings of, 62–63, 73
orientation of new, 44, 58
performance criteria for, 65
personnel records of, 67–69, 78–80
physical environment and, 113–16, 120–22
professional development of, 70–71, 81–84
recognition of, 67
salaries of, 43, 66–67, 88
scheduling, 44, 57
state requirements for, 40
substitute, 44–45, 59
supervising, 66–67
termination of, 47, 66
training of, 63–64, 74–76
Staff-child ratio, 40
Start-up costs, 86
State licensing and certification agencies, 225–30
Statements
of goals, 12, 19
of philosophy, 12, 13, 21–22
of purposes, 12, 20
State requirements
for accident and emergency policies, 142, 143, 149–50
building regulations, 112–13, 118
for child care plan, 126–28, 137–39
for children's records, 129, 140
for communicating with parents, 176–78
for health policies, 144, 151–52
for licensing, 214, 225–30
for staffing, 40
for training of staff, 63–64
State unemployment insurance, 94
Students
evaluating performance of, 4, 8
role in cooperative learning group, 3–5
Substitute staff, 44–45, 59
Summative evaluation, 212
Supervision of staff members, 66–67
Supplies, 86–87, 88, 97–100, 245–48

T

Tax-exempt status, 94
Tax returns
annual, 94

quarterly, 93, 94
Teacher, defined, 5. *See also* Staff
Telephones, 143, 199, 204
Termination of staff members, 47, 66
Texas
on emergency policies, 143
training requirements of, 63
Toddlers
caring for, 13
curriculum planning for, 125, 126
environment rating scale for, 114, 213
information for parents of, 177, 180
nutrition for, 158, 170
physical environment of, 114, 115
Training of staff, 63–64, 74–76

U

Underweight children, 159
Unemployment insurance, 94
U.S. Department of Agriculture (USDA), 93, 156
U.S. Department of Education, 156
Utah, materials list of, 86

V

Virginia
on communicating with parents, 176–77
training requirements of, 63
Visiting day, 199
Volunteers, 40, 181

W

W-2 forms, 94
W-4 forms, 94
Water area, materials list for, 247
Water table, materials list for, 247
Withholding exemption certificates, 94
Woodworking, materials list for, 248
Written records. *See* Records

Y

Young Children, 33